John A. Redhead

GETTING TO

Know

God

and other sermons

ABINGDON PRESS
New York • *Nashville*

GETTING TO KNOW GOD

Copyright MCMLIV by Pierce & Washabaugh

Library of Congress Catalog Card Number: 54-5230

An earlier version of the sermon "The Love of God" appeared in *Here
Is My Method,* edited by Donald Macleod and published by the Fleming
H. Revell Co., and is copyright 1952 by John A. Redhead.

SET UP, PRINTED, AND BOUND BY THE
PARTHENON PRESS, AT NASHVILLE
TENNESSEE, UNITED STATES OF AMERICA

CONTENTS

Getting to Know God

"I have called you friends."
—John 15:15

It was my pleasure once to visit a certain college campus during religious emphasis week. When I met with the officers of the student association to ask their advice as to what themes they thought should be presented, I received from them only one suggestion: "We feel a sense of unreality in our religious life," they said. "Please tell us how to find God real."

Shortly after that I was talking with an older person who said: "I am facing a crisis in my life. I have never paid much attention to religion, but now I need something stronger than myself to lean on. Yet I cannot seem to make contact with God. I do not know where to look for him. I cannot get my hands on him. So I am coming to join the church and see if there is anything here to help."

When Robert Browning was asked what sentiment expressed in his poetry best represented his deepest conviction, he answered: "I am very sure of God." How little like Browning, how much like these others, are we! If only there were some signpost that could put us on the track of a real experience of God!

Well, what things in your experience are real to you? You can judge the reality of anything by its influence on you. In the light of that test friendship will prove to be about as real as anything you can think of.

Elizabeth Barrett Browning said to Charles Kingsley: "What, sir, is the secret of your life? Tell me, that I may make mine beautiful too."

"Madam," Kingsley answered, "I had a friend."

When you look back into your life, you will discover that most things of which you are proudest have been put there by your friends—whether that friend is your mother in the home, your roommate in college, or your associate in business or in the church. Tested by their influence on us, our friends are perhaps the most real experience we know.

Now put that fact alongside Jesus' words, "I have called you friends." He is telling us that God is our friend. If God is our friend, then religion is friendship with God. With some of us this insight has been the most rewarding of all truths. It has opened doors hitherto closed. It is the key to what we seek—the experience of getting to know God.

I

Note, for one thing, that it puts a handle into our hands. We have all wanted this experience of getting to know God, and did not know where to begin. But this is something we all know how to use.

Here is a man who says: "When I go to church and listen to the sermon, it all sounds reasonable enough. But when I get home, I feel like a man in a rowboat in the middle of the ocean without any oars."

That is just the trouble about religion—there doesn't seem to be any handle to take hold of. Start out to learn to play golf, and there is the handle of the club to take hold of. Start out to learn to drive a car, and there is the wheel of the car to take hold of. Start out to learn to knit, and there are the needles and the yarn to take hold of. But start out to learn how to be religious, and what have you got? Well, if you've got hold of the idea that religion is friendship with God, then you have in your hands a handle by which you can throw your experience into gear and begin moving.

The handle is simply this: If your religion is friendship with God, then those same laws which govern your relationship with your friends will apply in your relationship with God.

Great friendships do not just happen. They have to be built, and there are certain well-defined laws which govern their building. If, then, we can discover the ways human friendships are set up and kept going, and then put those same laws to work for divine friendship, we can expect results. That is the meaning of law in this sense. Supply the conditions and results will follow. Lower water to a temperature of thirty-two degrees and it will freeze. That is the law. Meet the conditions which the laws of friendship demand and results will come. That is the law.

II

Walk through a second door into our truth and see that these laws are as familiar as two and two. The first is the law of *association,* which says simply that the friends who are most real to you are those with whom you associate most.

Some years ago you had a friend who lived next door. You saw him practically every day. You hunted and fished together. You played golf together. You advised together about your flowers. You were with him some part of every day. You felt close to him. The influence of his life on yours was something that was real. Then he moved away. At first you corresponded and visited back and forth on week ends. But now another neighbor has moved in, and you do not see your former neighbor as much as you once did. While you still count him your friend, the influence of his life on yours is not as marked as once it was. Back of that fact is the simple law of association, which says that if two people are to be real to each other, they must take time to be together.

That does not mean that you need to see him every day. It

9

does not mean that you need ever to have seen him. Charles E. Jefferson said once, "I feel as if I know Paul better than any man who ever lived." You wonder whether that could be when nineteen centuries separated the men. But Jefferson tells us: "I made Paul my daily companion. I read his letters over and over again. I read everything I could find which has been written about Paul; I have thought about him and talked about him, so now I feel as if I know Paul better than I know any other man who ever lived."

So you can fulfill the law of association in your friendship with God even though you have never seen him. If you want to know George Washington better, what do you do? You go to the library and get a book about him and sit down and read it. If you want to spend some time with God in order to know him better, why not do the same thing? Why not get a book about him and sit down and read it? You say the world and its affairs are so much more real to you than God is. Well, how much time did you spend yesterday with the world and its affairs by means of your newspaper? And how much, by comparison, did you spend with God in the pages of his Book? Do you begin to see why it is that those folk who make a place for the Bible in their schedule of reading usually show the marks of knowing God?

There is another time-honored method of fulfilling the law of association—not only the habit of meeting God in the pages of his Book but face to face in what we call prayer. Someone asked a little boy if he said his prayers every night, and he answered, "No sir, some nights I don't want anything." Well, if we have tested out prayer in its truest sense, we have learned it is not so much a way of getting things from God as of getting God into our natures. It is being at home to God, having open house for the Almighty, showing hospitality to the Most High.

There is a second law of friendship, as fundamental as the first—the law of *expression*. It means that friendship feeds on

10

the expression of regard that one feels for another. We are so made that no thought, no feeling, no impulse is fully ours until we have expressed it. The more frequent the expression, the more complete the possession. Speak of your love to your parents or to your children, tell your friend of your admiration, and the love and admiration become more real.

But friendship is expressed in deeds even more than in words. You can say it with words, and you ought to; but the words will become hollow unless sometimes you say it with flowers or candy. The gift you sent on Mother's Day has drawn you closer to your mother. The cake you baked for your neighbor who was entertaining guests has strengthened the neighborly bond. The tray you fixed and sent to your sick friend, the visit you paid to the hospital, the note of good cheer you sent to the faraway heart or hearth—these expressions of your friendship have brought you closer to your friend. As a mother sacrifices for her invalid child, her love for him grows. As you perform kindnesses for your friend, your interest in him deepens. By the same token, as you give expression to your friendship for God in kindness to his children, he becomes "closer than breathing and nearer than hands or feet."

It has never yet failed to work. Wherever you find a life that is lived in the service of men, you will find a person who knows God. The Schopenhauers, the George Eliots, the Robert Ingersolls may not believe in God. Of course not. They live apart, isolated. But ask William Booth, or Wilfred Grenfell, or Jane Addams, or Florence Nightingale, or Muriel Lester, whether or not they know God. Why, he is the most noticeable thing about their lives! Wherever you find a life which flings itself away in the service of people, there is a person to whom God becomes more real every passing hour.

These are the laws of friendship—the law of association and the law of expression. The one says that if two people are to be real to each other they must take time to be together. The other says our feeling for another becomes more real the more frequently we give expression to it. When you stop to consider the ways these laws apply on the horizontal plane of your human friendships, you can believe that they will work when you put them into operation on the vertical plane.

III

Now let's take a third step. We have begun feeling grateful that there is something so certain as a law in our dealings with God. Now that law turns round and says: "Very well, if you wish results, meet the conditions. It is your move first."

But we are human beings and naturally lazy. We are victims of the modern mood of wanting something for nothing. We are in search of push-button religion. We are like the woman who was being shown a new washing machine. The salesman spoke of all its good points, reminding her it would put an end to all backbreaking toil and give her more leisure to enjoy her children.

"And now, madam," he concluded, "all it takes is to push this button."

"Well," she wanted to know, "who is going to push the button for me?"

We are like that, are we not? We want to pay the preacher to do our praying for us. We want to let the Sunday-school teacher do our Bible reading for us. We want the Boy Scouts or the Community Chest to do our kind deeds for us.

You would like to know God as a person who is as real as your friend next door? Then do as much for your friendship with God. Put yourself in the way of seeing him more often. How long has it been since you met God in the pages of his Book or talked with him from your knees? Then take the Book of God, and more especially the New Testament, and more especially still the four Gospels, and there you will find one who can say, "He that hath seen me hath seen the Father." Walk with him and talk with him; listen to him and linger with him. And then let your love begin to speak the language

12

of deeds. How long has it been since you went out of your way to do something for God? Not something for which you expected to be repaid. Not a dinner party for one who would return the favor. But a cup of cold water in his name, which no one but you and the thirsty soul knew of. Friendship isn't a game of solitaire. It takes two to play it, and it is your move.

Why not take some time right now to catch up on your part of the laws of friendship which have been too long neglected? Why not get out that Bible and dust it off and spend some time walking up and down its pages? While reading about the Samaritan who helped a needy traveler you will be reminded of someone who in his pilgrimage needs the help you can give. This very day is a good time to catch up on that sort of thing. When you come back from that kindness done, not in the name of self-interest but in the name of God, you will feel better inside than you have felt in a long time.

Read the New Testament and you will never doubt that God was more real to Jesus in the days of his flesh than to any person who ever lived. Of course Jesus was God; but there is a sense in which, as we are told, he increased in wisdom and stature, and in favor with God and man, just as we do. If you will read between the lines, you can put your finger on the laws which governed that growth. *As his custom was,* he entered into the synagogue, and read the scriptures. *As his custom was,* he went up into a mountain and prayed. *As his custom was,* he went about doing good.

It is not a matter of chance that the life which gave itself to these practices of the presence of God knew God as no other life has ever known him. One fact is related to the other as the law of cause and effect, and the law still stands today, as changeless as the character of God. Let a man take God as his friend, let him give himself in obedience to the laws of friendship, and it must follow as the night the day that he will discover that God is his friend, and that he is a rewarder of them that diligently seek him.

A God Who Grows

"And God said unto Moses, I will be that I will be."
—Exodus 3:14 (A.S.V. mg.)

The idea that God's a God who grows may startle you. Right away you say, "But how can God grow? Isn't he the same yesterday, today, and forever?" Well, let's see.

Look at what the text has to say about the matter. In the commonly used translation of the Bible known as the King James Version the answer to Moses reads, "I am that I am." However, in the margins of the several Revised Versions you will find other suggested readings. This means that the men who made the translations were not sure which one best suited the sense of the writer. One of them says, "I am, because I am"; another, "I am who I am"; and another, "I will be that I will be."

This last reading seems to fit best the circumstances out of which the words come. The children of Israel are being ground to dust under the heels of a hostile pharaoh in Egypt. God turns on a stop light in the burning bush and lays upon Moses the task of leading his people out of their bondage. Moses, however, is hesitant about accepting such a commission.

"Who am I, that I should go unto Pharaoh," he says, "and that I should bring forth the children of Israel out of Egypt?"

"Certainly I will be with thee," God answers.

This sermon was suggested by and is indebted for some of its thought to a sermon delivered some years ago by Ernest Trice Thompson.

Moses is not yet persuaded. He presents another difficulty.

"Behold," he says, "when I come unto the children of Israel, and shall say unto them, The God of your fathers hath sent me unto you, and they shall say to me, What is his name? what shall I say unto them?"

Remember that among the Hebrews the name of a person was supposed to reveal the character of that person. Simon was called Peter as a prophecy of the kind of man he was to become, a man who could stand like a rock. His name was a picture of his character. So it was that the name of God would reveal the character of God. Moses is fearful lest when he goes to his people he will not be able to enlighten them as to the character of the God who has sent him. He wants a name that will make the matter crystal clear. Therefore he says to God, "And they shall say to me, What is his name? What shall I say unto them?"

"I will be that I will be," is God's answer.

I

You know what God meant. He gave Moses a name which describes the divine character as that which, from time to time, his people would discover it to be. Each age would find out new facts.

"You ask me for a name which will fully describe my nature to the people?" God is saying. "I cannot give you that, because my nature is such that it cannot be fully described. But I can tell you this: As it is more and more completely unfolded, it will prove to be more than words can express."

God is too big to be shut up within the limits of mere words. A definition is a poor thing by which to know the kind of God with whom we have dealings. You go to God and say to him, "God, I want to know what you are like." And he says to you, "I'll not force you to be content with a mere explanation. I'll give you a demonstration in experience." To think you can start out on a trip that will take you all the way around the greatness of God, as a man travels around the earth, charting its seas and continents on his maps, is futile. Let a man know all of the divine nature which can be put into words; let him spend the rest of his life exploring the remainder; and when he comes to the end of his days, there will still be stretches of the divine love and power on which he has never set foot.

I like the way God replied to Moses. It was an answer which carried a challenge with it. "Go tell your people this: I am a God who grows. I possess a future tense. I stand before you as a great mountain. Set out to climb, and as you climb, each new height will open before you new visions of truth concerning my greatness and my grace. I do not say that I am what I am merely; or that I will be what I have been only; but that I will be what, from time to time, you prove me to be, as here and there your needs are met in me." It is, without a doubt, the picture of a God who grows.

II

Let us see what this growing God can do for us in helping us to understand some of the hard things in the Bible.

Surely your reading of the Old Testament has brought many questions to your mind. You have wondered how standards of conduct far below those which you set up for yourself could have been passed over without censure and apparently with the blessing of God. A teacher in our Sunday school said to me once, "I certainly do dread teaching the next several months." When I asked why, he said, "The lessons are from the Old Testament, and there are so many things there I do not understand." They say that after the death of Henry Drummond there were found among his papers letters from many honest inquirers who were perplexed about the Old Testament. The problem which bothered them most was that the ethical standards in its pages are so far below those of our generation.

For example, how can it be written in the 137th psalm: "Happy shall he be, that taketh and dasheth thy little ones against the stones"? Such sentiment seems poles apart from the prayer of our Lord on the cross: "Father, forgive them; for they know not what they do."

Or what will you say concerning the law in Deuteronomy which prescribes the treatment of a stubborn son? "If a man have a stubborn and rebellious son," it reads, "which will not obey the voice of his father, or the voice of his mother, and that, when they have chastened him, will not hearken unto them: then shall his father and his mother lay hold on him, and bring him out unto the elders of his city, and unto the gate of his place; and they shall say unto the elders of his city, This our son is stubborn and rebellious, he will not obey our voice. . . . And all the men of the place shall stone him with stones, that he die." Suppose two parents should obey that law today! Suppose they had a son who was stubborn and refused to obey them, and they should take him down to the city council, and the council should order that he be stoned to death!

Or take that law regarding the treatment of women captured in war. During World War I a town was captured, and a soldier asked his officer if he should deal with the prisoners as the Bible told him to. The officer, supposing the Bible would guarantee the best possible treatment, told him Yes. Then the soldier called to his attention this law in Deuteronomy: "When thou goest forth to war against thine enemies, . . . and thou hast taken them captive, and seest among the captives a beautiful woman, and . . . wouldest have her to thy wife; then . . . she shall be thy wife. And it shall be, if, thou have no delight in her, then thou shalt let her go whither she will." Here is a standard of conduct commanded in the Old Testament which is not even countenanced in modern warfare. What do you make of this difference in standards?

17

Some eighteen centuries ago there lived a man named Marcion who felt the force of this difficulty. He solved it by deciding that the God of the Old Testament must be a different God altogether from the God of the New Testament, and he persuaded many Christians of his day to follow him in abandoning the Old Testament. But such a solution is out of the question for us. Where, then, shall we look for help?

We need go no further than the truth wrapped up in our text. God did not promise that he would reveal himself all at once to his people. What he promised was that each new age would discover new truth. Here in the Bible we have a picture of the God who grows and grows, in the minds of men, till at last they see him complete in Christ. Here and there in the Old Testament we get a glimpse of the true character of God, and our knowledge grows bit by bit. Then when we get to Christ, all these bits are pieced together in him who is the "express image of" the Father.

Stanley Jones tells about a mother who was reading to her little girl the Old Testament account of the massacre of the Amalekites. The little girl was bothered. She could not understand how the God who told us in Christ to love our enemies could approve wholesale murder. So her mother told her that the people who lived back then did not know as much about God as we do—that now we have Christ. Her little face lighted up and she said: "Oh, yes, Mother, now I see. This back here was before God was a Christian."

God has always been a Christian. He does not change one iota in himself. He is the same yesterday, today, and forever. Yet God has changed in the pages of the Old Testament as men came closer to the full revelation of his character in Jesus Christ.

When Gamaliel Bradford began to write his book on Robert E. Lee, he approached his subject in a spirit of hostility. He had little sympathy with the South, and so at first he decided that the title of his book would be *Lee the Rebel*.

As he studied the material and came to know his man better, however, he decided that "rebel" was not quite the word he wanted; and so he changed to *Lee the Southerner*. After he read more and knew Lee still better, he decided that to call him "southerner" was also inadequate. Therefore he changed the title to the one by which you know his book: *Lee the American*. Even so the God who is described in Genesis as sending flood and fire to destroy men came to be "our Father" in the Gospels.

Instead, then, of discarding our Old Testament as being unworthy of the God of Christ, we see in its pages a picture of the God who grows; and we cherish it as the record of the fulfillment of the promise made to Moses, "I will be that I will be."

III

But all the gold is not yet gone from the rich vein of this promise of God. The past has not exhausted its meaning. It still stands for you and me to enjoy. It is God's word to us as we face the future. It says that "the half has never yet been told." There are riches, "exceeding abundant above all we can ask or think," yet to come. The God who grows will get bigger every year, as every year we find in him the answer to our needs.

That is the personal testimony of the man who first opened to me the meaning of this word of God. Professor Ernest Trice Thompson of Union Theological Seminary, Richmond, Virginia, puts it this way: "Sometimes I like to look at the old Bible my mother gave me when I joined the Church. I was nine years old at the time, and for many years I used to read that Bible and mark with a red pencil the verses which had some real meaning for my own life. As I read that Bible, I think again of what God meant to me as a boy. God meant more to me in high school than in grade school, more in college than in high school, more at the university than he did at college, although it was there that I almost lost him. I could not begin to tell you now what my Lord and Saviour means to me, but it is infinitely more than he did in those early years. And yet I know that I have hardly begun to appreciate the riches of his grace. I still live on the sunny side of life. I have never known the sorrows some have known. I have never known the temptations some have known. I cannot tell what the future holds. But I do know that whatever does come will only reveal to me new depths of his love and his power."

It was so with an aged saint F. W. Boreham tells of interviewing at her home in Australia.

"Ah, yes," she said, "I was only a girl when I entered into the sweetness of religion."

"You speak of the sweetness of religion as though it were a thing of long ago," said Boreham. "Do you mean it became exhausted?"

"Oh, well, you know," she replied, "the tone of one's life changes with the years. I left my girlhood behind me. I married. Children came into our home. Life became a battle instead of a frolic, and sometimes the struggle was almost grim." Then she told of having lost two sons within a single week, and later her husband.

"Do you mean then," asked Boreham, "that under the stress of all this sorrow you lost the sweetness of religion?"

"Under such conditions you would scarcely speak of sweetness," she said. "I would rather say that during those sterner years I entered into the power of religion. Only once did my faith really stagger. It was on the night of the second funeral, the second within a week. I was kneeling on the spot in my room where, morning and evening, I had knelt for many a day. But I could not pray. I felt that God had failed and forsaken me. And then, all at once, a hand seemed laid on my shoulder and a voice sounded in my ear. 'Am I a man that I should lie?' it said. I was startled. I was chastened and rebuked. Then a great peace soothed my broken spirit. No, I should not speak of sweetness as I recall those years of bitter sorrow and struggle. In those days I entered into the power of religion."

"Would you say," he asked, "that you now enjoy the sweetness or the power?"

"Now I have them both!" she exclaimed. "The sweetness that I knew in my English girlhood has come back to me in the days of my old age, and the power that came to me during the years of testing has never left me. Now, bless his name, I have them both!" [1]

The tragedy of our experience is that we live such little, listless, lifeless lives. We are so easily content to be less than our best, so willing to allow circumstances to roll over us and mash us flat, so weak in our acquiescence to being bullied by temptation. And all the while God stands by saying, "Come on! Strike hands with me, and I will show you depths in my love deeper than any you have ever seen, and heights of my power higher than any you have ever known. I will be all that you need me to be. I will go with you, and grow in you, till by and by life will begin to glow for you. I will be all of this, the sweetness and the power, if you will let me."

Will you?

[1] *The Uttermost Star,* ch. iv.

A Glimpse of God

"And the Lord passed by before him, and proclaimed, The Lord, the Lord God, merciful and gracious, . . . forgiving iniquity and transgression and sin, and that will by no means clear the guilty."   —EXODUS 34:6-7

Our text is one of the most remarkable verses in the whole range of Scripture. It is remarkable because, a way back near the dawn of our religious history, it gives us the essence of what God is like. As time went on, and as the face of God was unveiled in the person of his Son, the meaning of these words stood out in bolder relief. But even the only begotten Son, from the bosom of the Father, had nothing more final to say than is said in the words of our text.

I

Look at the dramatic circumstances in which they were spoken. We have just noticed how God placed on Moses the responsibility of leading his people out of their Egyptian slavery. When God called Moses and told him what he had in mind, Moses asked for a name—a name that would describe a character. God answered, "I will be that I will be"— meaning that he could not put the whole of his character into words, but that he would be proved to be all that his people needed him to be, as more and more their needs were met in him. On the basis of that promise Moses took the job and started out.

At Sinai, you remember, the people fall into idolatry and

bow down in worship before the golden calf set up by Aaron. God is angry, and says to Moses, "Let me alone, that my wrath may wax hot against them, and that I may consume them." Then Moses reveals his true character in an episode which stands out as one of the brightest on any page of history.

"Oh, this people have sinned a great sin," he says to God, ". . . yet now, if thou wilt forgive their sin—; and if not, blot me, I pray thee, out of thy book."

Moses is not only asking that God pardon their sin. He is pleading that, if someone must be punished, God will let the people live and lay the penalty for their sin on him. Human leadership can never rise higher than that.

Then Moses goes on with another question. He was willing to start on the basis of the blanket promise made at the burning bush. But this golden calf business—his people's sin, and God's anger, and the need of forgiveness—this all calls for something more definite in his knowledge of God. He must know more of what God is like if he is to lead people who keep a golden calf up their sleeve. So he repeats the question he asked at the beginning. Only this time, instead of saying, "Tell me thy name," he says, "Shew me now thy way, that I may know thee."

"All right," God says, "how about tomorrow morning? You come up the mountain by yourself, and I'll put you in a crevice in the rock and pass by so you can see me. I'll cover your face with my hand until I have passed by. Then I'll take away my hand, and you can see my back—only a part of me, because no man can know all there is to know of God."

I know Moses didn't sleep any that night. Could you sleep if you had a date with God tomorrow morning—if God had promised to tell you something he had never told anybody, something everybody wants to know, the answer to the question that means most to everybody? If you had a date like that, you couldn't wait for the time to come to keep it. And Moses couldn't either. The Book says that he rose up early in the morning and went up the mountain. His mind was full of the question that had kept him awake all night: "What's he like? Is he a policeman, waiting to arrest my people? Or a judge, his mouth watering to levy sentence? Or is he a moral weakling who only winks at wrongdoing? What's he like?"

Then the time comes. Moses looks out and sees a cloud— and whenever you see a cloud in the Old Testament, keep your eyes open, because God is close by. While Moses is standing in the crevice of the rock, the Lord passes by before him and proclaims: "The Lord, the Lord God, merciful and gracious, longsuffering, and abundant in goodness and truth, keeping mercy for thousands, forgiving iniquity and transgression and sin, and that will by no means clear the guilty; visiting the iniquity of the fathers upon the children, and upon the children's children, unto the third and to the fourth generation."

Well, that's it—that's the answer to the question of the ages. And the Book says that when Moses heard it he "bowed his head toward the earth, and worshipped."

When you and I take in the full meaning of the words, we will feel like doing the same. I have been reading a book that some say is the greatest work on theology published in our generation—*An Outline of Christian Theology* by William N. Clarke. It says that God is in essence Holy Love. It says that there are many things true about God— that he is good and kind and just and pure and faithful— but that all of these qualities are a part either of his holiness or of his love. Today the most we know about God is that he is Holy Love, yet that was exactly what God told Moses 3,500 years ago. There were many facts about God these people did not take in. They did not take in the full meaning of either his holiness or his love, and it took an Isaiah and his fellow prophets to make them see that this God is the only God there is and that his sway extends over the entire universe. Yet here we stand 3,500 years after God spoke to

Moses and we do not know any more about what the inner core of the character of God is like. As that truth dawns upon us, we too bow our heads toward the earth and worship. We stand in reverent awe before this glimpse of the Eternal God himself.

II

Let us take this word "holy" and see what it means for us. The holiness of God is his inward character of perfect goodness. If God is perfect goodness, and if his purpose is to produce that goodness in you and me, then he must take sides against all badness. You know the story about President Coolidge which tells about his coming home from church one day and being asked by his wife what the preacher talked about.

"Sin," he said.

"Well, what did he say about it?"

"He was against it."

And so is God. He cannot help being *against* it because he is *for* its opposite. That fact explains some of the words in the Bible which we have a hard time understanding. The Bible talks "our Father" and in the same breath speaks of the "wrath of God." That does not mean God loses his temper; it simply describes the reaction of his holiness toward sin. He is bound to be against it because of what he is. Or the Bible talks about God as being a "consuming fire." That does not mean that he is a God of caprice, one moment a Father and the next a consuming fire. It means that because he is a Father of perfect goodness, he cannot put up with badness— just as you cannot put up with anyone's making improper advances to your daughter.

In the light of that fact, then, we are ready to take in the meaning of one thing he said to Moses. He said: "The Lord, the Lord God, . . . that will by no means clear the guilty; visiting the iniquity of the fathers upon the children, and upon the children's children, unto the third and to the fourth generation." What he is saying is that, because he is holiness itself, he can never put up with anything that is unholy—that he not only cannot put up with it; he will not put up with it.

That means that you cannot break a law of God to save your life. You are a fool to try it because you will always be broken by it. For example, if you eat like a glutton, you may say you have broken the laws of health. But during those long days in the hospital you wake up to see that it is not the laws which are broken but you.

One day a senator stood with his back against the wall of the rotunda in the Capitol, and something fell and struck him on the head. A friend saw what had happened and rushed up to ask what he could do to help.

"Go into the Senate chamber," said the senator, "and have the law of gravitation repealed."

In like manner a boy went to confession, and the priest asked if he had learned the Ten Commandments. "Father, it's this way," he replied. "I was going to learn them, but I heard tell they were going to do away with them."

Well, you can just as easily repeal the law of gravitation as you can do away with the Ten Commandments. Both of them are built into the structure of this universe, and the working of one is as true as the working of the other. So a man is just a plain dunce who tries to beat the law of God. "The Lord, the Lord God, . . . that will by no means clear the guilty."

III

Yet in this glimpse of God we see something else also. We see alongside the holiness of God the love of God. "The Lord, the Lord God, merciful and gracious, longsuffering, and abundant in goodness and truth, keeping mercy for thousands, forgiving iniquity and transgression and sin."

A woman took a friend with her when she went to a photographer to have her picture made. The beauty parlor had done its best for her. She took her seat in the studio and fixed her pose, while the photographer was adjusting his lights. Just before he pressed his bulb she said to him, "Now be sure to do me justice." The friend said, with a twinkle in her eye, "My dear, what you need is not justice but mercy."

Sometimes we feel imposed on by the universe and say to ourselves, "There's no justice in the world." We think that if only we could receive our just deserts, we would ask for nothing more. Well, the holiness of God guarantees justice. As the letter to the Hebrews says, "God is not unfair; he will not forget what you have done." (Moffatt.) But suppose there were justice in God and nothing more. Suppose we got what we deserve and only what we deserve. What would be your score with God on that basis?

The English author J. H. Shorthouse as a young man found trouble believing Christian truth because he did not feel any need of forgiveness. In his trouble he went to see the saintly Bishop of Lincoln, Edward King. The bishop did not argue but suggested that he do a rather strange thing. He gave him two sheets of paper, one plain white and the other with a black edge all around it. The bishop told Shorthouse to take the two sheets home and write down on the white sheet everything he had ever done that was absolutely good with no touch of evil, and on the black-edged sheet everything in his life that had been bad, sinful, and wicked. Shorthouse went away and in a few days came back.

"That black-edged sheet is filled on both sides," he said. "It was filled in five minutes, and I could have filled a dozen more like it. On the white sheet I wrote down just one thing, the only good thing I have ever had in my life—my love for my mother. But on second thought I rubbed even that out, because too often it had been marred by selfishness."

"What did you do then?" the bishop asked.

27

"Then I got down on my knees and said, 'God, be merciful to me a sinner.' "

What we need is not justice but mercy. And the text tells us that what we need we have: "The Lord, the Lord God, merciful and gracious, longsuffering, and abundant in goodness and truth." He will not clear the guilty—no, because when your child puts his finger into the fire it will be burned. No matter how much you love him you cannot banish the burn. But you can forgive him. You can tell him that, even though he disobeyed you by playing with fire, now that he is sorry for his disobedience you will forgive him and not hold it against him any more. It is thus that, while God is forced to visit our iniquity on us, he is still merciful and gracious and forgiving.

When one person wrongs another, he sets up a barrier between them. But when you love somebody, you cannot stand for anything to come between you. If your child has disobeyed you and goes to bed with a sense of guilt on his conscience, you cannot sleep. You get up and go into his room, and the troubled look on his face hurts you. You tell him how much you love him. You tell him you love him enough to forgive, that your tears will melt down the barrier which stands between you. Now you can go to sleep, because you have made up.

Is it too much to say that God can't sleep some nights because, like disobedient children, we have put a wall between us, a wall of separation?

There are some people who stay away from church because their consciences hurt them, because they are ashamed to go where they think God will see them. There are some people who do not pray because they fear to call the attention of a holy God to their guilty hearts. If you have felt like this, take courage and draw near to the God who, if we but glimpse him, is seen as "The Lord, the Lord God, merciful and

28

gracious, . . . abundant in goodness, . . . forgiving iniquity and transgression and sin." Draw near and behold his portrait in the only begotten Son who said, "Him that cometh to me I will in no wise cast out."

Will you come?

IV

Looking at God Through Christ

"He that hath seen me hath seen the Father."
—JOHN 14:9

An American tourist was traveling in Europe. When he went to the desk to pay his hotel bill, the cashier asked if he wished to wait for a receipt.

"No, thank you," he said. "If God wills, I will be back here next week and you can give it to me then."

"Do you still believe in God?" asked the cashier.

"Why, of course," said the tourist, "don't you?"

"Oh, no," he answered. "Over here we gave that up a long time ago."

"In that case," replied the traveler, "I believe I will wait for my receipt."

It makes a big difference with you whether you believe in God and, more particularly, what kind of God you believe in. What you believe about God is the pivotal fact of your experience, for it determines what you believe about life and duty and destiny.

For long years God tried to teach his people how to spell his name. He gave one syllable to Moses, and another to Isaiah, and another to Jeremiah. Finally he spoke again, and when the Word was made flesh the full name of God was spoken. The letter to the Hebrews puts it this way: The Son is "the express image of his person." In other words, Jesus is the epitome of God. He reaches out and gathers up within himself all that the seers and prophets of old had been trying to say about God. He himself sums up the whole truth when he says in our text: "He that hath seen me hath seen the Father." So when you look at God through Christ, you can be sure you are seeing God as he is.

Suppose you had a ten-year-old boy, and he came and asked you what God is like. From your reading of the Gospels and your understanding of Christ you would want to explain God in terms of the needs of his own life. How would you go about it? What is "the Father of our Lord Jesus Christ" in relation to experience? Just exactly where does he fit in? I think we can put the matter in three simple phrases.

I

For one thing, God is a Father whose love *never lets us down*. Take Christ as the authorized spokesman of God, what he said as the truth about God, what he did as the life of God, and there can be no gainsaying this first fact. In his life here on the earth Jesus did not go around letting folks down. Rather did he go about lifting them up. He taught people to believe in God as the great Dependable, as the one above all they could count on.

Now there are times, of course, when it seems that God lets us down. We pray for a passing grade on an examination and do not get it. We pray for a job and it goes to the other fellow. We ask to be delivered from some crippling handicap but remain handcuffed to it. We seek a detour around the road with a cross at the end of it, but find all other roads are closed. Sometimes it does seem as if God lets us down. It even seemed so to his own Son once. "My God, my God," he cried, "why hast thou forsaken me?"

And all the while the reason for our thinking so is our self-centeredness. We put ourselves at the center of the universe and expect God to regard us as such, to make it his chief business to look after us. We count him our private property—our personal nursemaid, if you will, who has nothing else to do but to watch our interests and save us from trouble. And so whenever we mash our finger, or have a flat tire, the cry goes up that God has let us down.

That is to misunderstand God. God never promised to save anybody from trouble, not even his own Son. We are not the center of the universe. God is the center. His eternal purpose, not our personal pleasure, is the big thing.

But though God never promised to save anybody from trouble, he does promise to save us *in* trouble. That is a promise you can count on, and it will not let you down. He "preparest a table before me in the presence of mine enemies." That reminds us of a word which war put into our vocabulary —"logistics." It means the service by which fighting forces are kept supplied with what they need to do battle. God has a service of supply too, and with respect to logistics you can know that God never lets you down.

One day a man stopped me on the street to tell me about a letter he had received from his son in the army. The boy was on one of the foreign battlefronts, and he was writing to encourage his father. He knew his father was suffering what seemed to be more than his share of trouble, and he also knew that there would probably be more to come. But he said just the right thing in his letter—I could tell it had had its effect on the father. What the boy said is what I am seeking to say: "Dad, I know you've had to take a lot lately. But remember— God never overloads anybody! He gives you power to pull whatever he puts on you."

That is something to remember: God never overloads you. The Father we see through Jesus Christ always gives strength equal to the struggle. He is a Father who never lets you down.

II

But we are always in danger of committing libel against God unless we go on to say a second thing. Though God's love never lets us down, it also *never lets us off*.

The love of God is not soft like a jellyfish. It has backbone. It is built on certain standards, and when those standards are not met, the penalty falls heavy and sure. God is a Father whose love never lets us off. The God who never lets us down is also the God of moral holiness.

Our forefathers had much to say about the wrath of God, about that quality in the divine character which demands that sin be punished. Jonathan Edwards pictured so vividly the dangers of a sinner in the hands of an angry God that women fainted and strong men clung to the pillars of the church in agony. You have not heard a sermon on hell like that in a long time. We have given up that sort of imagery—and rightly so. But in giving up the imagery we are in danger of losing sight of a truth which we can lose sight of only with great peril—that there is something in God which requires that sin be punished, something which makes it impossible for us ever to do wrong and get by without having to pay for it.

There are people who are telling us that we need to get back into our thinking these sterner truths about God. They are saying that we have watered down our belief, and made God a sort of soft, sentimental "Yes-Man," who winks at sin and says it doesn't matter. So much so that somebody says of him, "God will forgive, all right. That's his business."

But anyone who looks at God through the eyes of Christ knows that along with the tenderness of God goes also the terror of God. It is not that God finds any pleasure in punishing sin. It is just that there is something in God called holiness, and that holiness sets up a law which says that right is right and wrong is wrong, and wrong must be punished. Not even God can repeal that law.

Jesus called God Father, but he never called him an overindulgent grandmother. He called him a righteous Father, one whose love is built on certain standards so that he can never let down the bars. Who was it said, "Be not deceived;

33

God is not mocked: for whatsoever a man soweth, that shall he also reap." Somebody wanted to know what that means. You know what it means. It means that hang-overs always come on the morning after. It means that the man who sows his wild oats will have his outcome tax to pay. It means that punishment is tied to sin like the burned spot to the blaze. It means that if a man eats salt herring not even the grace of God can keep him from getting thirsty. It means that not even God can give a man a pass that will let him through the gates of sin without paying the price. It means that while God is always compassionate toward the sinner, he is never complacent about the sin. It means that while God is a Father whose love never lets us down, he is also a Father whose love cannot let us off.

III

But the story about God must always be a continued story until a third thing is said. He never lets us down. That is a word of strength for the man who is in deep water. He never lets us off. That is a word of warning for the man who would play fast and loose with sin, deluding himself with the false fancy that he can get away with it. But furthermore—God is a Father whose love *never lets us go*. That is a word of hope for the man who thinks he is past all hope.

Here is the greatest word that can be spoken about love. It keeps on loving in spite of everything. It takes no account of the wrongs done against it. No matter how often its offers are spurned, no matter how often its favors are refused, no matter how poignantly it is wounded or how far away the loved one wanders, it always holds on, never gives up, never lets go.

When you look at God through Christ, this is the one thing you see standing out above all others. You remember when our Lord was criticized by self-righteous Pharisees for associating with people like the publicans and sinners, who were considered outcasts. He answered them by telling three little stories. A woman lost a piece of money—a poor woman who couldn't afford to lose even a penny—so she went through the house, moving the chairs and tables, taking out the rug and sweeping out every dark corner, looking for the coin. God is like that woman. A shepherd had a hundred sheep, and when one strayed and was lost, the shepherd left the flock and went out on the mountains wild and high, seeking until he found. God is like that shepherd. A father had a son. The son showed himself ungrateful for his father's favor, turned his back on his father, went out to a far country and threw his life away. But that father always kept his candle burning in the window, and always kept watch too. One day there is a speck down the road. Gradually it gets larger. It comes nearer. "It walks like my son! It is my son!" Down the stairs, through the open door, out through the gate—"when he was yet a great way off, his father . . . ran, and fell on his neck, and kissed him." God, says Jesus, is like that father.

In the First World War, Harry Lauder, the Scottish comedian, lost two of his sons in action. After the war was over Lauder's physicians recommended a long rest for his tense nerves. From England he went to Australia's quiet, and there he spent most of his time taking long walks and making new friends. Late one afternoon he started out on a long walk with a very young boy who had become a close companion. They passed several homes where service banners hung in the windows.

"What are those?" asked the boy.

"Each star in a banner means a son went from that home to the war," Mr. Lauder told him.

"And why are some of the stars gold?" the young friend asked.

"That means the son did not come back. He was killed in the war," the man answered.

They walked on in silence. The street opened into a road. The sky grew darker. A star twinkled. The boy pointed to it.

"Did God send a son to the war too?" he asked.

"Yes," Mr. Lauder answered thoughtfully, "God sent his only Son to the greatest war ever fought, the war against sin, and it cost his life."

The sure test of love is always the length to which it is willing to go. Let no one feel that he has sinned away his chance, that the door is shut in his face. For the gold star of God's only Son, embroidered on the service banner in the window of heaven, attests a love that has gone all-out to seek and to save.

He never lets us down. No, and he never lets us off. But, bless his holy name—and this is the real gospel—he never, never, never lets us go. He is seeking now, seeking you and seeking me. Your business, and mine, is to allow ourselves to be found.

Will you?

V

Pathways to God

u shalt love the Lord thy God with all thy heart, and
all thy soul, and with all thy mind, and with all thy
gth."   —Mark 12:30

Our thought takes its starting point from a problem that
worries many people. They are sincere in their devotion to
God, and yet they are troubled when they find that their experience does not follow the right pattern—at least what they
have somehow been led to believe is the right pattern. Perhaps
the answer to their anxiety lies in the fact that there are
different patterns, that there are various pathways to God.

Our Lord himself opens the door for such a fact in his
phrasing of the Great Commandment. For the sake of a
questioning critic he is outlining the duty God requires of
man, and he puts it this way: "Thou shalt love the Lord
thy God with all thy heart, and with all thy soul, and with
all thy mind, and with all thy strength."

Our religion is the response of our personality to the personality of God. Inasmuch as our personality is composed of
mind and heart and will, our religion is therefore our thought
of God, our feeling toward God, and our conduct in relation
to God. It is the response of the parts of our personality to
God.

But we differ in the make-up of our personalities. Few and
far between are those who possess a perfect blending of mind
and heart and will, of thought and feeling and acting. Most

of us are weighted more heavily in one faculty than in the others. We are predominantly either emotional, intellectual, or volitional, according as our natures are stronger in the feeling, thinking, or willing faculties.

Because our religion is the response of our personalities to God, it is natural that our experiences differ. We can't help being ourselves, and to try to force our experiences into other molds or patterns would be both unnatural and artificial. No man need try to copy another, for if he is sincere, he is just as religious in his own way as another in his. In the words of the text Jesus is pointing out to us several pathways that lead to God, and each of us may find here the right way for himself.

I

The first pathway is meant for the person who feels his religion. "Thou shalt love the Lord thy God," Jesus says, "with all thy heart." The heart is the seat of emotion, the center of feeling. Those of us who are more emotional than intellectual or volitional find that our experience of God is more heavily weighted on the side of feeling than on the sides of willing or doing.

Fortunate for us that it is so! What we all are after in our religious experience is a sense of its reality, and there is no better way for a person to be convinced that something is real than to feel it. Someone asked Mel Trotter how he knew he had been converted, and he answered, "I was there when it happened." When God stepped into his life, the experience was so emotionally vivid that it could be dated. Many of us envy the folk who are equipped with such a ready sense of reality in things spiritual.

Emotion in religion is a good thing. We simply could not get along without it. You can see the kinship between the words "emotion" and "motive" and "motor." The motor in

38

your car is the thing that makes it go. Motive in your life is the same thing, and back of motive is emotion.

As a matter of fact, we get our word "enthusiasm," which means fervent feeling, by adding together two words that mean literally "in God." A person who has enthusiasm is a person who has God in him.

That is probably news to some of us who have got so sophisticated that we are more concerned with dignity than with feeling in our worship. I remember having heard of an old-timer who strayed into a church where the ushers wore striped trousers and morning coats. He became deeply moved by the sermon, and it was only natural that he should give forth with a fervent "Amen!" The man immediately became the object of disapproving glances. The reaction led him to decide he would remain quiet. But soon he was lost in enthusiasm, and another "Amen" came out. The head usher shook his head, and once again the visitor made a good resolution. But once more he was carried away by the earnestness of the discourse.

"Hallelujah! Praise the Lord!" he said.

Whereupon someone touched him on the shoulder and said, "Sorry, sir, you can't do that in this church."

I suppose we will go right on being dignified, yet one cannot help wishing that sometimes a few old-timers would stray in and help us put a little feeling into singing the praise of God.

But the man who feels his religion is not the person we are concerned about now. He carries with him the assurance that his pathway leads to God, and we need waste no sympathy on him.

II

There are others of us who deserve more consideration—for example, the man who responds to God chiefly by his thinking apparatus. He is not devoid of feeling any more than the man of feeling is devoid of thought, but his nature is more intellectual than emotional. So he is simply being true to himself when he follows Jesus' instruction to love God "with all thy mind."

For example, I remember a student at Salem College. We were having a discussion on religion in one of these informal gatherings when students take you back behind the scenes and let you know what is going on in their minds. This girl had a problem on her mind.

"I have always been led to believe," she said, "that when I accepted Christ and became a Christian, it would make a big difference in my feelings—that I would always feel good and wouldn't have any trouble being good. But it hasn't worked out that way. I believe that I am a Christian, but I have never felt like jumping up and shouting, 'Hallelujah!' When I check on myself, I am sure I am being perfectly honest in believing in God and committing myself to Christ. And yet it troubles me that I don't feel the way some folks say they feel. It makes me wonder if my religion is genuine. Now, that's my problem. What is your answer?"

Of course the only answer is that there are different pathways to God. She was a victim of the revivalism of the past. The sudden and emotional conversion is so much more dramatic than any other that it has been pictured by some as the only genuine conversion. When this student, who thought her religion, found that it didn't conform to the pattern she supposed was authentic, she began to question the validity of her experience. When she was reminded that conversion can be just as genuine if gradual, just as authentic if intellectual, she seemed to feel better. Yet that is one of the liabilities of the intellectual in religion: he lacks the sense of authenticity with which feeling always stamps a thing.

Furthermore, the thinker is miserable as long as he is unable to fit the facts of his faith into the pattern of logical consistency. The emotionalist is never troubled by logic. The fact that two and two do not always add up to four in matters of faith never dampens the ardor of his hallelujah. But the man whose response to God is mainly by way of his mind can never be happy until he has pieced this jigsaw puzzle together.

Yet there is one asset which the man of thought has over the man of feeling: once he works out his faith, it is more constant. The man who majors on emotion is subject to the fluctuations of feeling. One day he is on the mountaintop and next day down in the valley. One day he is David singing, "Praise the Lord"; the next he is Elijah sighing, "It is enough; now, O Lord, take away my life." The man of emotion is the man of moods in religion. But while the man of thought can never reach as high in ecstasy, neither will he descend as low in despair. When the sun shines he is not quite so ready as his friend to burst into song, but when the sun fails to shine neither is he so quick to jump into the river. His faith is more constant, and he can sing with Stevenson: "I believe in an ultimate decency of things; aye, and if I woke in hell, should still believe it."

III

But there is another pathway that most of us will recognize as opening up especially for us. For, in addition to the heart and mind, Jesus tells us we are to love God with all our soul and all our strength. The word "soul" speaks of the volitional nature, our will; and the word "strength" of the physical energy with which we work out a purpose determined upon by the will. In short, to love God with soul and strength is to put the emphasis on the doing of the will of God. This third pathway is for the practical man in religion, and he is in the big majority with us. Most of us are neither feelers nor thinkers in religion. We look askance at those folk who get too excited, and we have neither time nor talent to occupy our minds with the subtleties of hair-splitting in theology.

We take our religion out in doing. We love God with our wills and our strength. And while we will not have the enjoyment which either the feeler or the thinker has, yet as doers we are on much safer ground.

The person whose experience is mainly feeling does certainly enjoy his religion. It becomes for him a kind of intoxicant. There was an Irishman named Peter Bray who was converted, and who went overboard with all the fervency of the Irish. "It's a wonderful feeling," he said. "I go walking down the street. When I lift my left foot it says, 'Glory!' And when I lift my right foot it says, 'Hallelujah!' " But there is a danger against which this man must always keep on guard. It is so easy to take all our religion out in feeling. There was the shallow soil on which the seeds fell and, because there was no depth of earth, sprang up and quickly withered away. We have all seen the man who is converted all over again every summer at revival time. He needs to be reconverted, because his religion does not last longer than the enthusiasm of the meeting. He goes up like a skyrocket and comes down like a stick. In comparison, his brother who is the practical man in religion does not get nearly so excited at revival time, but he does decide to join the church and do his part. While he does not get any big kick out of paying his tithe, yet the treasurer will tell you that his checks keep coming.

And the thinker in religion—he gets his thrill too, the thrill of adventure, of intellectual gymnastics. He can sit up all night in a religious "bull session," arguing as to how many angels can sit comfortably on the head of a pin. He gets a tremendous kick out of trying to devise devious arguments to justify the ways of God to men. But, being the panel-discussioner in religion, he is open to the danger of all panel discussioners—the danger of thinking a thing all the way through, and then of doing absolutely nothing about it. The thinker in religion must be always on his guard lest he rest content in thought. He may think his way into a perfectly

42

logical faith and profess his belief in Jesus Christ as Lord; and yet this same Jesus stands up and says to him: "Not every one that saith unto me, Lord, Lord, shall enter the kingdom of heaven; but he that doeth the will of my Father which is in heaven."

"He that doeth!" The pedestrian plodder, this practical man who takes his religion out in doing the things it says, albeit he lacks the thrill his more emotional and intellectual brothers get, somehow seems to get farther up the road.

Furthermore, there is an additional advantage on your side if you choose to be a doer: you can always find the pathway along which to travel to an experience of God. For example, look at yourself lying in bed in the morning. As long as you rely on feeling you will never get up. You simply do not feel like it, and hard as you try to work up a feeling, it simply does not come. Neither can you think yourself into getting up. That mind of yours can find many arguments for keeping you in bed: you were up late last night, and it wouldn't do any good to get up because, even if you went to class or to the office, your mind wouldn't work, so why not sleep late and catch up, and then you will be fresh for your work? You simply cannot get yourself out of bed on the basis of feeling or thinking. What do you do? You bring your will into play and force yourself to get up. And by the time you've had your shower and your coffee you are feeling fine and your mind is ready for a good day's work.

So it is in religious experience. If you have never been able to get emotional about this faith of ours and you sit there waiting until you can feel its reality before you commit yourself to it, you will never get anywhere. Or if you wait until your mind can fit the puzzle together and you can find a creed that answers all your questions, you will keep on sitting. You've got to put that will to work. You've got to get up and start walking, even though you see but one step. As you do, the light will open up the way ahead, and the exercise will enliven your feeling tone. It is mighty, mighty hard to feel your way or to think your way into being a Christian. But any man can live his way. For, said Jesus, "if any man will *do* his will"—will do as much of the will of God as he is sure of—"if any man will do his will, he shall know of the doctrine."

If you are dissatisfied with what goes for the experience of religion in your life, minor on feeling and thinking for a while and major on doing. Begin to love God more devotedly with your will and your strength. Take the commandments of Christ and give them a flesh-and-blood setting at home with the family and at the office with the force. Begin to catch up on the things you are behind with at church. Never let a day pass without doing what you know is your duty. Find someone who needs a little kindness and give it. Make up your mind to go all-out for God, giving a totalitarian response to his totalitarian demand. Do these things and you will know—you will *know*—that God *is,* and that he is "a rewarder of them that diligently seek him."

VI

The Wisdom of God

"O the depth of the riches both of the wisdom and knowledge of God!"   —ROMANS 11:33

One of the young men in our church, who was leaving soon for military service, came by to see me. He was kind enough to give me a little visit with him before he left. After we had talked about when he was leaving, and where he was going, I gave him a picture of his church to carry with him, and then said: "What about your religious faith? Is it in good shape as you get ready to shove off, in case you might need it before you get back?"

I have thought often since of his answer. It went much deeper than you might expect.

"Yes," he said, "I believe in God, and I believe God knows what he is doing. Of course I have asked all the questions. But when I am honest I must believe that a certain Intelligence has been at work around here before we men came on the scene. The very fact that plants give off the oxygen that people need to breathe in order to live, and that people provide the carbon dioxide which plants need, says to me that there must be somewhere a Mind above this whole thing. That Mind is God."

He said some other things, but let us stop with his starting point. It seems to me that he put his finger on a bit of truth we might chew on with profit.

He said, for example, that behind matter there is Mind, that behind instinct there is Intelligence, that behind sensation there is Sense, that behind war there is Wisdom, that behind this puzzle there is Purpose. This is the faith that fills the Bible from beginning to end. The wonder of it so floods the mind of the Apostle that it bursts out in the words of the text: "O the depth of the riches," he cries, "both of the wisdom and knowledge of God!" Let us see now what this faith has to say to us.

I

For one thing, it provides an interpretation of facts that puts meaning into your life. As Harry Emerson Fosdick used to say, no fact is the whole of itself; the rest of it is the meaning you place on it. What, for example, is a kiss? Well, you can go to your dictionary and get the facts. There you will discover that a kiss is "to smack with pursed lips (a compression of the closed cavity of the mouth giving a slight sound when the rounded contact of the lips with one another is broken)." So that is what a kiss is! But when you stop to think of what happens when two lovers meet, or when you welcome your son or daughter home after a year away at school, you see that such a definition leaves most of the story untold. No fact is the whole of itself; the rest of it is the meaning you place on it.

The meaning multitudes are placing on life, in these days when so many of us are forgetting the fact of God, is a far from flattering one. A few years ago a college paper offered a prize for the best definition of life. Here are a few entries that won honorable mention: "Life is a joke which isn't even funny"; "Life is a jail sentence which we get for the crime of being born"; "Life is a disease for which the only cure is death." We might laugh this off as just a bit of sophomoric sputtering, except that it is of a piece with much that is being said by more mature minds. There are those who are telling us, for example, that man is only a "forked radish," "a sick fly taking a dizzy ride on this gigantic flywheel," and that life is only

> A tale
> Told by an idiot, full of sound and fury,
> Signifying nothing.

The flaw in such an interpretation is that life does not work well on the basis of it. A few years ago a brilliant newspaperman went into a hotel room in New York City and took his own life, leaving behind this note: "No one is responsible for this except myself. I have run from house to house, from country to country, from wife to wife, in a vain endeavor to get away from myself. I have done what I have done because I am fed up with the necessity of inventing devices for getting through twenty-four hours a day." That is a picture of what happens when life has no high meaning, no noble purpose. It goes to pieces in your very hands! It cracks up under your very eyes!

But move over into the New Testament and see what a different air you breathe. Once you look the Son of God full in the face, you can never think meanly of yourself again. Listen to him as he talks to you about who you are. You are not a forked radish; you are an offspring of the Almighty. You are not a sick fly; you are the tadpole of an archangel. You are not a mass of dancing dirt, come from nowhere, going nowhere; you are a child of God, filled with the Spirit of God, and placed upon this earth to do the will of God. It makes a lot of difference what you think of yourself. If you consider yourself an orphan of the apes, the chances are you will spend your time making a monkey of yourself. If you think of yourself as a child of God, you will make it your business to be like Christ.

And so when I think of our young friend going away into

military service, I think of what his faith in the infinite Wisdom means to him. I see him on his way back to base some night, telling himself that his life is worth nothing and it would not be wasted if he threw it away on an hour's debauch. Then this truth sounds like a trumpet and calls him to attention, saying, "You were not made for this. *There* is your destiny." A light flashes in the distance. Once more he puts his feet in the upward path, and begins again to climb!

II

Move on now and notice a second meaning of our truth. As our young friend left home and went away, what could his faith in God as intelligent Mind say to him about this world?

He faces, as all of us face, the possibility of catastrophe. He sees a dictator at the head of a nation which officially declares that there is no God, which flies in the face of all we believe and flouts the values, like freedom, that we hold dear. What he sees makes him wonder. Is this world going anywhere worth going, or will the march of time get lost in the dark? Is there any use fighting and dying in a losing battle? Is God any match for the devil?

Then he thinks again of the intelligent ordering of life whereby plants and people mutually support each other, and he sees behind such design a Designer. He says to himself that God is no fool. He says that God must know what he is about in this world.

And then he begins to think of his history. He remembers that the wisdom of the race has coined a proverb to the effect that "the mills of God grind slowly, yet they grind exceeding small." He thinks of the Kaiser in the First World War, and of Mussolini and Hitler, and what happened to them in the Second World War. He sees that the throne of power in this world is not big enough for two. Then, the more he thinks about it, the more he is impressed by the fact that there seems to be something in the nature of law running through this world, something which says that evil is self-defeating. He seems to remember having read somewhere that "whatsoever a man soweth, that shall he also reap." He thinks of the movies he has seen whose moral is that crime doesn't pay. He remembers that the motto of the Northwest Mounted Police is something about always getting their man. He thinks of the boys he has known in school who bragged about breaking the Ten Commandments, and now he sees what actually happened: the Commandments still stand, but the boys themselves are beginning to break. The more he thinks, the more respect he comes to have for God.

And then all of a sudden he wakes up to this fact: If God made this world, and if he has any sense at all, he would be sure to fix it so that things will never get out of hand. He remembers that that is exactly what the Bible has been saying all the time. He begins to see the meaning in a verse he had never understood before, which quoted Jesus as saying, "I beheld Satan as lightning fall from heaven." That marvelous mind of our Lord penetrated so deeply into the nature of things that he saw in his crystal ball the devil already done for —whipped, beaten, "fallen . . . from heaven." Then our friend gains another insight from the Bible. He remembers that, whereas Satan breaks out in Genesis, and seems to ride high, wide, and handsome, swinging with his rights and lefts in that running battle with God from Genesis to Revelation, yet in the last book in the Bible, where do we leave him? We leave him hog-tied, hand and foot, licking his burns in the lake of fire and brimstone.

Martin Luther had no easy time of it, you know. Once when his enemies had ganged up on him and seemed to be getting the better of him, he was mighty blue. Next morning when he came downstairs for breakfast he found his wife, Katherine, all dressed in black and her face draped in mourning.

"What's this?" asked Luther. "Who's dead?"

"God," she said without looking up.

"Who said so?"

"Well," she said, coming to life, "from the way you've been moping around the place the last few days, everybody would think so!"

It was rebuke enough for the reformer, and he went back to win the war of the Reformation.

III

There is yet a third meaning of our friend's faith in God as intelligent Mind which he might find useful to take with him. If we cannot always find the answer to all of our questions, it means something to believe that there is an answer, and God knows it, and sometime he'll make it plain. Meanwhile we can trust where we cannot see.

Take just one of those questions, the one which towers above all the rest—Why? It is possible that our young friend in military service is making friends right now in camp. Suppose that later on one of these friends, who is as fine a boy as you'll find anywhere, meets with disaster in his plane and his life is snuffed out. Why? Why—if God is good, and values goodness in people—why does he permit good boys like this one to be taken away from a world which needs them so badly, while some who would appear to be more expendable are left?

It is the same old question which rises up to plague us so often. Why, if God is just, is there so much injustice in the world? Why, if God is powerful enough to do all his holy will, does he not put the dictators in their places and lay forever the scourge of war? What sense is there in things like cancer, and snakes, and storms, and droughts? "My God, my God, why hast thou forsaken me?"

Well, I wish I had the answer, but I don't. Yet it helps me to bear the anguish of the "why" to believe that God is no fool, that he knows what he is doing, that there is an answer. Sometimes I have difficulty understanding what some people do, for it is easy to misinterpret and to misjudge. Then when I learn more of the facts it all becomes plain. "If I had only known!" Haven't you said that a hundred times?

Well, if only we knew more of the mind of God! So often a few additional facts change the whole picture. But our knowledge is limited. As one man puts it, we are like an insect crawling up a column of the Parthenon. We know no more of the eternal plan of God than that insect knows of the architecture of the building. Yet we have this advantage over the insect: we can find evidences of a plan, and we know there must be an answer somewhere to the parts of the plan which are not clear to us. Meanwhile we can trust where we cannot see.

Some years ago in a mine disaster in England forty miners lost their lives. The families of the men gathered about the entrance to the mine, grief-stricken and bewildered. Someone asked Bishop Edward Stanley to say something that would help these hapless folk, and this is what he said: "We stand today in the face of mystery, but I want to tell you about something I have at home. It is a bookmark, embroidered in silk by my mother and given me many years ago. On one side the threads are crossed and re-crossed in wild confusion, and looking at it you would think it had been done by someone with no idea of what he was doing. But when I turn it over I see the words beautifully worked in silken threads, 'God Is Love.' Now, we are looking at this tragedy from one side, and it does not make sense. Someday we shall be permitted to read its meaning from the other side. Meanwhile let us wait and trust."

It helps to trust—to assure ourselves that God is no fool, that he knows what he is doing, and that sometime we'll understand.

Meanwhile, the trusting heart! Meanwhile, the faithful life!

VII

The Love of God

"God commendeth his love toward us, in that, while we were yet sinners, Christ died for us."   —ROMANS 5:8

In reading the Bible we find much about God as intelligent Mind. But we are bound to be struck even more by the emphasis on God as one who loves. What does this mean for us —this truth that at the heart of things there is a heart that loves?

Any good teacher will tell you that one of the principles of learning is apperception—which means that we learn on the basis of what we already know. Now "love" is a word which has its place in our daily speech. We know something about it. We love our mothers and fathers, our brothers and sisters, our sons and daughters, our wife or husband or sweetheart. On the basis of what we know about love on the human level, therefore, let us explore the meaning of this love divine.

I

For one thing, it is the nature of love as we know it to desire the highest good of the one who is loved.

The young lover thinks constantly of his beloved and spends his time devising means of pleasing her. When he buys a box of candy for her, he remembers her taste for nuts or soft centers; and when he sends her a corsage, he considers the color of the dress she will wear. He thinks of the time when they will be married, and he saves his pennies to buy a vacuum cleaner in order to spare her the monotony of the broom. He wants her to be happy, and no task is too great if it is for her good.

The wife holds the same desire for her husband. She prepares the dishes he likes and browns the toast and drips the coffee to his taste. If his health is uncertain, she will go to no end of trouble to watch his diet. She wants him to succeed in his business; and if his hours demands it, she will get up early to give him his breakfast and stay up late to keep his supper warm. She wishes him to be happy, and for her too no task is too great if it is for his good.

The mother holds the same desire for her child. If she hears him sneeze in the night, she will get out in the coldest weather and put the covers on him. She wants him to grow up to be a healthy person, and so she spends her time studying the kind of food he needs, and sits for hours at the table coaxing him to eat. She wants him to grow up to be a person of fine character; and so when she finds he has told her a lie, knowing that such conduct cannot go unnoticed, that he must be disciplined, she washes his mouth out with soap or gives him a spanking. She tells him that the punishment hurts her more than it hurts him; he finds it difficult to believe, but she knows whereof she speaks. She punishes herself only because of her love for her child, which makes her want him to grow up to be an honest man. It is the nature of love to desire the highest good of the one who is loved.

Now take that truth with which we are so familiar in our human loves, lift it up to its highest level, and you will begin to get some idea of what love in God is. Paul says that God presses home his love for us in the cross. The motive behind that cross was only and always God's desire for our highest good. "God so loved the world that he gave his Son, that whosoever believes in him might have life." Life is the best thing God has to give. God wants you to have health of body and mind and spirit. God wants you to be free from the things which harm your life and the life of your home, the things that we call sins. God wants you to have the happiness which comes from living harmoniously with other people and with himself. And God wants you to have the life which is eternal, which goes on living forever.

Moreover, that same love lies back of some of the things we find it difficult to understand. Just as the mother's love made it necessary to punish her child for disobeying her, so the love of God desires so much the highest good of his people that sometimes he must resort to discipline: "Whom the Lord loveth he chasteneth."

This, then, is one of the meanings of love in God. God wants you to be happy and healthy and wholesome. If you could get up every morning and say to yourself, "God desires the best for me today and is willing to help me to have it," you would be well on the way to having a good day.

II

Take another step into our truth and see that it is the nature of love to be willing to give itself to the loved one in order to impart that highest good. There is a difference between wanting a person to have some good thing and being willing to give up something yourself—or to give yourself—in order that he may have it. But real love never stops short at desires; it is always willing to go the length of sacrifice.

That is a fact with which we are familiar on the human level. The young lover wants his beloved to be happy, and he knows she likes to go to football games; so he gives up buying a new tie or a new hat in order to get tickets.

Your wife wants you to get on in the world as fast as you can; so she pinches pennies at home, doing the washing instead of sending it to the laundry, in order to put the money back into the business.

Your mother paid the price of suffering to give you birth,

and all your life your mother and father give up things to give you the best in advantage. They want you to have an education, and so they think nothing of forcing the old suit, already shiny in spots, to go another season, or of making over last year's hat. One who sees what goes on behind the scenes when money is not too plentiful, and schooling is getting higher and higher in cost, knows there are many ways in which love is giving itself to keep this boy or that girl in school. You know, certainly, this truth about love: that it belongs to its very nature to give itself in behalf of the loved one.

Your knowledge of that truth makes it all the easier for you to step up to an understanding of the meaning of that fact in God. It is not something which wraps itself up in selfish isolation, expressing a desire for the good of you and me, but refusing to do anything to make that good possible.

God does not say: "I hope you will get along all right, but there is nothing I can do to help you. I wish you might be free from the hell of a guilty conscience, and strong enough to overcome the kind of living which places the load upon you. You have disobeyed my plain laws, and got yourself lost in the consequences of your own disobedience, and you will have to get out the best way you can. There is one thing I might do to restore the friendship you have broken by your waywardness. I could give my Son to bring you back. But that would cost too much. He would have to go the length of dying on a cross, and I couldn't stand that. No, the laws of justice demand that, having enjoyed the dance, you must pay the fiddler."

If God said that he wouldn't be God. You could see through him as you can see through the boy who wrote his girl friend: "My dear, I want to tell you how much I love you. I love you so much I would climb the highest mountain to sit by your side. I love you so much I would cross the widest sea to look into your eyes. I love you so much I would brave the fiercest storm to hold your hand in mine. Good-by for now, my love. I'll see you Saturday night if it doesn't rain."

But "God commendeth his love"—proves it, presses it home —"toward us, in that, while we were yet sinners, Christ died for us."

They tell us that on the southern border of the empire of Cyrus there lived a great chieftain named Cagular who tore to shreds and completely defeated the various detachments of Cyrus' army sent to subdue him. Finally the emperor, amassing his whole army, marched down, surrounded Cagular, captured him, and brought him to the capital for trial and execution. On the day of the trial he and his family were brought to the judgment chamber—Cagular, a fine looking man of more than six feet, with clear complexion and fearless blue eyes; his wife, a noble woman, worthy mate of such a man; and two children, with golden ringlets hanging around their bright, childish faces. So impressed was Cyrus with the appearance of the four that he said to Cagular: "What would you do should I spare your life?"

"Your Majesty, if you spared my life I would return to my home and remain your obedient servant as long as I live."

"What would you do if I spared the lives of your children?"

"Your Majesty, if you spared the lives of my children I would gather my scattered horde, place your banner above them, and lead them to victory on every field."

"What would you do if I spared the life of your wife?"

"Your Majesty, if you spared the life of my wife, I would die for you."

So moved was the emperor that he freed them all and returned Cagular to his province to act as governor thereof. Upon arriving at their little home, Cagular gathered his little family around the fireside which they never expected to see again.

"Did you notice," he said to his wife, "the marble at the entrance of the palace of the emperor—the different colors
56

matching with one another and the figures so perfectly formed?"

"I did not notice the marble at the entrance of the palace," she replied.

"Did you notice the tapestry on the wall as we went down the corridor into the throne room? The figures were as natural as if alive, and the colors blended as the rays of the evening sunset."

"I did not notice the tapestry on the wall in the corridor leading to the throne room."

"Surely you noticed the chair on which the emperor sat. It seemed that it must have been carved from one lump of pure gold, and with such skill of craftsmanship as I've never seen before."

"I did not notice the golden chair on which the emperor sat in the throne room."

"Well," said Cagular in surprise, "what did you see as we stood before the emperor on the day of judgment?"

"I beheld only the face of the man who said he would die for me."

Whenever you and I look up, we are looking into the face of the God who not only said he would die for us but did it. The test of love is always the length to which it will go. "Greater love hath no man than this, that a man lay down his life for his friends." There is something here that gets us. Whenever you stand face to face with the Cross, you cannot help taking off your hat, and getting down on your knees, and bowing your head in wonder before the greatness and the graciousness of the love of God. And yet God could not have done otherwise if he is love, for it is the nature of love to give itself.

III

We have discovered that love is a desire for the highest good and a willingness to give itself for the loved one. There is yet one more thing to be said. It is the nature of love to want to possess its object.

We are familiar with this fact also in our love on the human level. One of the surest signs of real love between you and your boy friend is a genuine pleasure in his mere presence. You want to be together. You are happy with him, and you are unhappy when you are away from him. If you keep him in your thoughts, wondering where he is and what he is doing all the time you are not with him, and living for the time when you can be together again, then you can put down your feeling as the beginning of real love.

So also it is with the love of a mother for her child. She wants to possess, and she sees her child leave home with a heavy heart. Sometimes the desire to possess overbalances the desire for the good of the child. Then mother love becomes smother love, when it refuses to give up its child to go away to school, to get married, or to take his rightful place as a person in the world. Love is a combination of two impulses: to give itself for the other, and to have the other for itself. Perfect love is the proper balance between those two impulses: to give and to share for the other, and to have and to hold for itself.

See, then, what it means when you turn the light of this fact upon the love of God. That cross on Golgotha stands forever as our proof that God was willing to go the full length in giving himself. Yet that willingness to give himself is also coupled with the desire to possess. The Son of Man came to seek, and the purpose of that seeking is that he might find, and bring back his people to God; for it is the nature of love to desire to possess.

So then the whole point of this thing is that God is looking for you. He is looking for you today. He is looking for you because he wants to find you and invite you to come back home so you and he can be together.

When you stop to think about it, you will know something

58

of how he feels. You send your boy or girl away to school in September, and from that moment you are looking forward to Thanksgiving. The big reason you want Thanksgiving to come is that your boy or girl will be coming home. You enjoy his letters, but that is not like having him at home. You love him, and because you love him you want to see him, you want to be with him, you want to have him at home with you.

You know too how you would feel about one who left home under a cloud; whose leaving left a scar doubly hard to take because it was unclean. You know how you would give anything to see him, and what a Thanksgiving any day would be if it brought him home. You would know then something of what is in the heart of God.

Stanley Jones tells of a girl who wandered away from home, was lost in the life of a great city, and ended in a house of shame. Her mother heard of what had happened and, with a heavy heart, went out to find her. She took some of her own photographs with her, and left one in each of the houses she visited. The girl came in one day, glanced carelessly at the picture on the mantelpiece, and came nearer. What she saw made her turn pale. It was the picture of her own mother, and on it were written the words, "Come home," signed "Mother." She fled the place, and there was a glad homecoming that night.

I wonder if you have ever seen a picture of God. I have. I can see him now in my mind's eye. His name is Jesus Christ, and all over the picture are written the words, "Come home."

Just think what a Thanksgiving there would be in the heart of God if you would answer that invitation in the words of the hymn we love to sing:

> Just as I am! Thy love unknown
>   Hath broken every barrier down;
> Now, to be Thine, yea, Thine alone,
>   O Lamb of God, I come!

VIII

The Will of God

"For I came down from heaven, not to do mine own will,
but the will of him that sent me."   —JOHN 6:38

A college student told me that the only permanently interesting subject in dormitory bull sessions is religion. My
guess is that the most fascinating part of these discussions
is God.

In our attempts to get to know him we have looked at
two of the sides of his nature. We saw that God is intelligent
Mind, and sought to discover the meanings that fact has for us.
Then we saw that God is not only a Mind that knows but a
Heart that loves, and explored the meanings of love.

But personality, whether human or divine, is composed not
alone of mind and heart. It has will also. The Bible is filled
with the fact of the will of God. You find it on almost every
page. Our Lord says in our text: "I came down from heaven,
not to do mine own will, but the will of him that sent me."
So we set ourselves now to discover some of the meanings of
the fact that in the nature of God there is will. What does that
fact have to say to us?

I

It says, for one thing, that in the will of God you can find
a guide for your life. Here is something which holds good for
long- and short-range needs.

Take the long-range first. Of the three major decisions

which every man has to make—Master, mate, and mission—probably the most difficult is the last. A lot of people have trouble making up their minds what they are going to do with their lives.

In the light of that fact, is there any source from which we might expect guidance in a matter so important? I believe there is, and I think we get the cue in our text. Our Lord says, "I came down from heaven, not to do mine own will, but the will of him that sent me." In other words, Jesus regarded his life's work as something which had been chosen for him by the will of his Father. It is not stretching the truth a bit to say that the very same thing can apply to every one of us.

A hundred years ago a man named Horace Bushnell preached a sermon which is still being reprinted and read today. It is called "Every Man's Life a Plan of God." The very title expresses a truth which would mean everything to many of us if only we could get it into our minds in time. It says that in the will of God there is a plan for you and me, and that we will reach our highest usefulness and deepest happiness only as we find and follow that plan.

So much for the long-range. There is a short-range guidance which we can receive also from the will of God. John R. Mott spoke of the will of God as his North Star. By that he meant that here was something by which he was constantly taking his bearings.

The most difficult thing you have to do is to make decisions. To go or not to go, to buy or not to buy, to accept this new job or to decline? As long as you are undecided you are miserable. Sometimes even after you have made your decision you ruin your happiness by worrying over whether or not it was the better one.

In making your decision you need some rule to go by, some yardstick, some test. You can do no better than to make the will of God your North Star. Whenever you have some question to settle, shut your eyes and see yourself in the presence of Christ. Put the matter to him. Then wait for a while—sleep on it, as we say—and give him time to speak. When you feel that the leading is unmistakable, go ahead.

One of the big advantages in making the will of God your North Star is that, once you get your answer, you know it is the right answer, and you lose no time in regretting your decision.

Some years ago a man, after having made a decision fundamental in his own life and that of his family, was miserable with the fear that perhaps he had made a mistake. A friend saw what was happening and spoke to him about it.

"You prayed about it," he said, "and you did what you believed to be the will of God, didn't you?"

"Yes."

"Well," he said, "that's all there is to it."

From that moment the man lost no more sleep.

It is out of its meaning in actual experience that I bring you the will of God as your North Star in both your long- and short-range needs.

II

Move on now and notice the meaning of the will of God in quite another sense—in its relation to the trouble which comes to us.

It is important that we give mature thought to this question now, for when tragedy strikes it is difficult to think straight because feelings are so upset. Our only real security is in God, and we want to have a faith so well grounded in the truth that no shock can shake us loose.

So then, suppose it comes. Suppose the one you love most dearly—your wife, your husband, your boy, your girl—is taken away. Your friends are kind in their friendship, and yet their help cannot reach all the way down, where it hurts. It takes God to do that. So you try to find some help by telling yourself that it was the will of God. But you can't, for the life of you, see why it should be. If you are the submissive type, you try to let it go at that, afraid to ask any questions for fear that God cannot stand an investigation without having to resign. In that case you cross your fingers when you say your creed about "God the Father" and hold on to a faith which is a way of believing something you know is not true. Or if you are not the submissive type, and somebody tries to tell you that the loss of your loved one is the will of God, then you decide you do not want to have anything further to do with a God like that. And yet, after you have given God his walking papers, you are still hungry for something. What is it?

It is the real truth about the will of God, which we must describe in two ways. First, there is God's will of desire. Studdert-Kennedy went to see a mother in England just after she had received the message that her son had been killed in the First World War.

"God took my boy," she said.

"No, never—not in the way you mean it," he answered. "To say that God took him is only half the truth. God took him only after the evil of men, organized in modern war, had put him to death. But to say that it was God's desire, God's intention, God's wish that he die—that is a lie."

And it is. It is if you take the word of Christ about it, for he makes it as plain as words can say it that "it is not the will of your Father . . . , that one . . . should perish."

Yet in addition to God's will of desire is God's will of purpose. It is his purpose that we learn to live together as brothers and sisters in one big happy human family. He has given each of us a free will, so that we are men and not manikins, persons and not puppets. We can misuse our freedom and get into a family fight, which is what a war is. When we do, we will get hurt. But God counts our freedom so important a thing that he respects it and will not override it, even though a war is the result. God's will is governed by that heart of love which desires that not a single loved one of yours should perish in the tragedy of war. Yet for the time being he must deny himself his will of desire for the sake of his will of purpose.

Whenever you bump into a question about the ways of God which is hard to understand, it helps to go back to the fact that Jesus calls God a Father. Ask yourself what you as a father would do if you were in his place. Here is one picture which helps some of us: As a father you want your son to learn to roller skate. That is your will of purpose for him. You place the skates on his shoes and send him out on the floor of the rink. All of a sudden his feet go out from under him and he sits down on the floor with a thud that shakes the building. You know it hurts him, and whatever hurts him hurts you. It is not your will of desire that he get bumped. But it is your will of purpose that he learn to skate; so for the time being you deny yourself your desire in order to achieve your purpose. When he falls you do not laugh at him with a cruel laughter which enjoys his misfortune. You go to him, pick him up and rub the hurt away, set him back on his feet, and encourage him with a steadying hand and a word of assurance. God, says Jesus, is a Father.

Our Lord did not like what men did to him. He prayed against it: "O my Father, if it be possible, let this cup pass from me." Yet when trouble came he did not turn his back on his Father. He accepted his cross as a part of God's will of purpose, and he found in his Father's friendship a source of strength which saw him through. With a willing co-operation in his Father's purpose he used his cross so that even today it is our symbol of redemption. Paul says it is for us to fill up what is lacking in the sufferings of Christ. When you use your cross as a part of his cross, it is still a cross, yet it is encircled with a crown.

III

Move on now and notice that there is another meaning for us in this fact. It means that God's will is a good will, that he wills only good for you both "in this present time, and in the world to come." Our Lord said, "I came down from heaven, not to do mine own will, but the will of him that sent me." That will is that all who believe "should not perish, but have everlasting life."

When Hannibal was born, his father, pagan though he was, took the baby to the shrine of his god and, holding him up in his hands, made this prayer: "O God, make him a better man than his father was."

Every parent among you has done the same thing. When your child was born, and even before he was born, you had certain hopes for him. When he was a mere babe you lifted your prayer to God for his future well-being. When he was old enough you took him to the sacred place that is your church to claim the promise of God to help you give him the things he needed to grow into a fine person. All during those happy years when as a toddler he played about the house and climbed on your knees you dreamed your dreams for his future. When you looked at him you saw, not the child he was, but the man you wanted him to become, taking his place in the life of the world and making his contribution to mankind's happiness.

Then when he went away to college you sat down and wrote him a letter, and you said something like this: "My son, ever since you came to live in our home as a tiny bundle of human flesh, your mother and I have had our hopes for you. We desire, of course, that you find happiness, and be useful. We want you to choose your vocation, prepare yourself for it, and achieve whatever success hard work will bring. But, above all, we want you to be a man, a real man, a Christian man—a man who puts character above all else. Your mother and I want you to know that we are your friends, and will always stand by to give whatever help we can in the achievement of this purpose for your life."

If, as a child, you were conscious of such a purpose on the part of your parents, you know what it meant to you. It set you going in a certain direction. It helped you to hold your course when you were tempted to stray off. Above all, it gave you the sense of backing—the feeling that there were others beside yourself who had your best interests at heart and were pulling for you.

Now we have on very good authority that it is altogether right to think of God from the point of view of parents. The name by which we know him best is Father. We are told that when we think of the best human father there is, God is better than that. "If ye then, being evil, know how to give good gifts unto your children, how much more shall your Father which is in heaven." Not until you can think of yourself as desiring something less than the best for your child, either in this life or in the world to come, have you any right to suppose that the will of God desires less than the best for you. If you miss the good purpose God has for you, either in time or in eternity, it is no one's fault but your own. For, as our Lord himself put it, "Him that cometh to me I will in no wise cast out."

That is what the artist Holman Hunt has told us in his painting called "The Light of the World." You have seen it and been impressed by it: the door of the human soul, and in front of it the Christ standing with a lantern in his hand—a vivid portrayal of our Lord's word: "Behold, I stand at the door and knock: if any man hear my voice, and open the door, I will come in to him."

The story is that when he had finished his picture he invited a few close friends to the studio for a preview. The curtain was drawn, and a gasp of admiration broke from the group. Then one of the men spoke up and asked Hunt if he hadn't left something out. "There's no latch on the door," he said. The artist did not wish to embarrass his guest, but he was forced to suggest that the man had missed the point of the whole thing. This is the door of the human heart, and the latch is always on the inside. It must be lifted from within, if it is lifted at all. "Behold, I stand at the door, and knock: if any man . . . open the door . . ." If!

Election day is set in the Constitution as the Tuesday following the first Monday in November. But every day is Election Day with God. In his eternal will there is a place prepared for every man and woman, every boy and girl who walk this earth. A single vote will elect you to that good destiny, and you are the only one who can cast it.

How, then, do you vote?

IX

The Power of God

"But we preach Christ crucified, . . . the power of God."
—I CORINTHIANS 1:23-24

On September 3, 1939, Great Britain declared war against Germany. That happened to be Sunday, and that morning the telephone rang at the church. A woman's voice said, "I want to ask you a question: If I had the power to stop war and did not, what would you think of me? Now," she went on, "for weeks many of us have been praying that war might be averted. We believe God is almighty, that he has power to do anything; and we have been praying that he would not let war come. But here it has come. It has almost staggered my faith, and I would like to have an answer to my question."

Quite often we find ourselves bumping into that problem in various ways. Here is a church which is split wide open, and a family in which brothers and sisters do not speak to one another, and a husband who is ruining not only himself but his wife and his children by his foolhardiness. Why doesn't God take the people in that church or that family and bump their heads together? Why doesn't he do something about that husband? If he is almighty he could do it, and if he is all-good he would do it. But we have prayed, and he does nothing!

Now if we had to choose between faith in the power of God and faith in the goodness of God, all of us would take the latter. We prefer to believe that God would like to prevent evil even if he lacked the power, rather than to believe that he could prevent it and refused to do so. For we believe goodness is more Godlike than almightiness. We ourselves have enough of goodness in us to hate evil and want to see it conquered; and if we thought there were less goodness in God than in ourselves, we could no longer bow down before such a god. He would be more devil than divine.

So the answer to our problem hinges on our thought about the power of God, and the proposition we confront seems to be this: Either God lacks power, or his power is something other than we have been accustomed to think of it as being. We prefer the latter alternative, and so our business will be to rethink our ideas of power in terms of the mind of God.

I

We begin by looking at what power means. A noted British theologian, Herbert H. Farmer, discusses this question in his book *Things Not Seen;* and he points out the truth that power means ability to achieve purpose. If you have the ability to do what you want to do, what you intend to do, what it is your purpose to do, then you have all power. If you do not have the ability to achieve what it is your purpose to achieve, even though you have at your disposal a million horsepower of force, then you lack power. For example, a bull is a powerful animal for plowing a field, but for the purpose of preserving delicate antiques in a china shop he is not powerful at all. The gentle hands of a frail woman would be power for that purpose. A locomotive engine is powerful for the purpose of pulling a train, but not for the purpose of teaching a child his alphabet. A gun is a powerful instrument for the killing of an enemy, but for the purpose of taking two men on the opposite sides in a war and making friends of them it has no power at all. Power is ability to achieve purpose.

This truth may show up a little more clearly in a picture that Leslie Weatherhead gives to us. Here is a man with a wife who was not very strong, but who always imagined she

69

was far worse than she was and complained accordingly. The husband was a very strong man physically, and at first he gave in to her. He used to carry her from room to room or, if she wished, out into the yard in the shade. Of course the woman got worse and worse. She became a doll. He had to go lift her and carry her everywhere. One day the husband, after taking the advice of competent persons, made up his mind that she was really quite able to walk out into the garden by herself. So he made her do it. He had to stand back and watch her stumble. In a sense he had the power to save her from falling, but it was his purpose that she learn to walk. It was therefore the exercise of a greater power to stand away. To intervene would have been weakness. To refrain was power. Again and again she complained. Again and again it would have been far easier to carry her. But his new purpose demanded a greater expression of power, even though he suffered something akin to anguish as he saw her fall. At last because he exercised his greater power she was cured, her character was strengthened, and happiness was produced which would have been impossible otherwise.

Now God is like that husband. He could step in and keep us out of trouble. But if he did, his act would be an expression, not of power, but of weakness. It would not achieve but would deny his purpose. As long as God has the ability to do what he wants to do, what he intends to do, what it is his purpose to do, then he has the only kind of power that is worth the name. That is power sufficient to constitute him God.

II

If we are to believe in the power of God then, we must understand the purpose of God. Christ has made it plain that the goal toward which God is working is the setting up of his Kingdom. God's purpose is to fashion a world of men, by the freedom of their own wills, into sonship to himself and brotherhood with one another. The Bible tells us God "hath made of one blood all nations of men for to dwell on all the face of the earth." All folks, then, are kinfolks; and what God is after is that we should realize our kinship. We know what a family is. We prize our family; we rejoice in our family. We live together as father, mother, brothers, sisters. We do not steal from one another, fight and kill one another. We love one another, not because we are forced to love, but because we want to love. And what God is after is a world of men who will live as a family, as sons and daughters of himself, and brothers and sisters of one another.

In the carrying out of that purpose God has imposed a limitation upon himself. He chose that we should have free will and the power to misuse it. It is his purpose to have a world of persons and not of puppets. He chose to make us with a free will by which we can choose to accept his purpose or reject it. It is a great risk that he took, but he thought the risk was worth while, for he wanted men and not machines. In other words, it is his purpose to deny his purposes until we can co-operate with him for their fulfillment. To say that is not to deny his power, for self-imposed limitations are an expression of power and not a denial of it. The husband who refrained from stepping in to save his wife from stumbling when she was learning to walk was giving evidence, not of his weakness, but of his power.

In the light of that fact, how could God step in and stop a quarrel without going back on himself? Suppose on that Sunday morning in 1939 God had walked up to Hitler and shoved a pistol into his side and said to him, "Put an end to this war or I will put you in jail. Call off your armies, give Poland her territory back, and make peace with the Allies, or I will lock you up." In the light of God's purpose that action would have been weakness and not power. For God's purpose is to set up his Kingdom, and the Kingdom of God is within you—in the minds and hearts and wills of people. If God wins there, he wins everywhere; if he loses there, he loses everywhere. With Hitler locked up in jail, still hating the Jews and wanting to fight the nations to build his empire, God would not have won. He would have lost. Nobody, not even God himself, can ever bully men into being brothers. The "big stick" as a weapon in spiritual warfare is never any good. Force is not power; it is weakness.

III

Power is ability to achieve purpose, and God's purpose is to set up his Kingdom. Does he have that power? I believe that he has, and I draw that faith from the Cross of Christ. For when methods of force are ruled out, there is only one method of winning such a victory, and that is simply to love—to love so utterly that even the most brutal and seemingly triumphant violence of sin leaves it still love; to suffer, and endure, and strive, and wait; to see hopes go down and desires temporarily frustrated; to take no short cuts; to attempt no violence; and thus to achieve the divine purpose in a divine way, and change hearts of men, even if it means the age-long bearing of a cross.

I know what you would say to God. You would say, "God, are you going to stand all that? What weakness!" But is it?

"Why, if I were God," one man said, "I would get a move on. I would lay about me. If I were on the throne, I would make some people's ears burn with boxing for their persistent neglect."

Yet when you turn to Paul you find that he does not share our common misunderstanding of the power of God. He says clearly that nothing is an expression of power which does not work toward the achievement of the divine purpose—the changing of men's hearts—and that the methods of violence, force, and coercion do not change men's hearts. So in the same sentence in which he talks about the cross he talks about the power of God. "We preach Christ crucified," he says, "unto the Jews a stumblingblock, and unto the Greeks foolishness; but unto them which are called, both Jews and Greeks, Christ the power of God." *Christ crucified, . . . the power of God!*

Strange, is it not? How can a man, even though he be the God-Man, nailed to a cross, ever be power? But look. Sin has done its worst. It has beaten him, bruised him, battered him, murdered him. What more can it do? Nothing. It has done all it can do. But what can the Christ do? He can still remain love. He can haunt the minds and consciences of men ever after. He can meet men in their thoughts, where no army can drive him out. He can lay hold of them in those moments when even sin and selfishness let down their guard, and confront them with the picture of one who prayed, "Father, forgive them; for they know not what they do." He can get into their blood and find hidden allies which will betray them into remorse, and send them out seeking for God, and falling on their knees before him, praying, "God be merciful to me a sinner." Yes, Paul is right. He points to the naked body of a deserted Christ hanging on a cross, and he says, "Christ crucified, . . . the power of God."

I suppose the last person in the world you would expect to find backing Paul in his claim is Napoleon. In his younger years he was the apostle of force. He thought God was always on the side of the biggest battalions. But he is older now, and wiser. Listen to him: "Caesar, Charlemagne, and I have founded empires. Upon what where these empires founded? Upon force, and they have crumbled into dust. Jesus alone founded his Kingdom upon love, and there are millions upon the earth today who do him honor." Wasn't he right? Where is Caesar, and where is Charlemagne, and where is Napoleon? They have all crawled off, and fallen down and died, and been buried in their narrow little graves. And where is Christ? Where is he? Well, he is all over the world, and the sun never sets on those who name his name. Paul was right. "Christ crucified, . . . the power of God."

And some day, bless his holy name, he is going to win all the way round. The kingdoms of this world shall become his, and machine guns will be found only in museums, and a multitude which no man can number, of all races and kindreds and peoples, will surround the Throne of the Lamb, and their song will be a hallelujah. I know it, because he said so. "And I, if I be lifted up from the earth, will draw all men unto me." There is only one condition—"if I be lifted up." That is your business and mine, to see to it that men see him there. And then God's power will be vindicated, for his purpose will be consummated. "All men—unto me!"

Do you believe that? If you do, and if you will begin to live on the basis of your belief, then God himself "shall see of the travail of his soul, and shall be satisfied."

X

The Providence of God

"We know that all things work together for good to them that love God." —ROMANS 8:28

If you are acquainted with the city of Charlotte, North Carolina, you may remember the time when you first tried to find your way around in the section of the city known as Myers Park. It is a jumble of streets which curve and cross one another with no apparent design.

Later on you discover that the key to the puzzle is a thoroughfare named Providence Road. Providence Road begins at Fourth Street and runs on out into the country. If you know where Providence Road is, you can pretty well find your way around. If you are looking for an address on Oxford Place, say, you consult your map and notice that Oxford Place turns to the right off Providence Road at the 1100 block, and there you are.

Now for many of us life is pretty much like the puzzle that is Myers Park. It looks like a jumble of streets that do not make sense, and a conglomeration of blind alleys that lead nowhere. Is there a Providence Road running through this map of life which can provide our cue?

Well, there might be. Where do you suppose Providence Road in Myers Park got its name? It got its name from the fact that it is the road which leads to a church out in the country named Providence. But where did Providence Church get its name? It got its name from its faith—its faith that there is a God behind this thing called life, that he is watching over us men and our world, and is guiding us toward the destination he has planned for us.

It is something of that faith which Paul put into the verse which gives us our text: "All things," he says, "work together for good to them that love God." Let us look, then, to see if there may be a Providence Road running through our Myers Park.

I

The first thing Paul says is that "all things work together." But do they? You look at the world through the columns of your morning paper, and then you look at the seemingly senseless happenings in your own experience. You see nothing that seems to work together according to any sort of plan, and you say to yourself, "That's just like the Bible—all wet, when you get down to brass tacks."

Then you come across something like this, from a man you know can be trusted. He is the late Robert Rainy of Scotland, and his name is known throughout the whole of Christendom. This is what he said: "There have been many happenings in my experience which I did not understand as I came along. Yet when I look back over my life I can see them working together according to something like a plan, which was above and beyond my own designing."

Or you turn to a book like the one many of you have read, *A Man Called Peter*. His wife says that after the death of his father and the remarriage of his mother Peter Marshall was unhappy at home and felt a consuming desire to escape to sea. At that time the British Navy signed boys at fifteen years and nine months. Peter was only fourteen, but he decided he would age a year and nine months overnight. For a year he had been taking exercises to stretch himself to the proper height. So he told his friends at school good-by, saying he was

76

leaving to join the navy. At dawn the next day he left home and went to the recruiting station, giving his age as fifteen.

But after only two days his true age was discovered, his parents refused to consent to a naval career, and he was right back where he started. He was so bitterly disappointed that he cried himself to sleep that night. Yet in the years that followed he looked back to see that "all things worked together" to keep him out of the navy and to bring him to America, where he found opportunity to prepare for his life's work.

When you look in the Bible, you find a man like Joseph, who was sold into slavery by his brothers, lied about by his master's wife, and thrown into jail. As a result of being in jail, he explained the king's dream, was made prime minister, and thus was in a position of power and able to supply food to his brothers when famine drove them down to Egypt. When his brothers stood before him, fearful of what his vengeance would do, he saw the Providence Road running through his tangled Myers Park, and he told them: "Ye thought evil against me; but God meant it unto good." When Paul wrote his letter to the Romans and told them that "all things work together," I can imagine Joseph leaning over the battlements of heaven and sounding off with a hearty Amen!

Look back into your own experience, and see if you cannot locate a Providence Road along which you have traveled. You were kept from straying off into some side street—marrying this person, entering that vocation, taking this job, going to that college. As you think of it, you can see now a guiding hand leading you on, above and beyond your own designing. So true is this fact that we have a proverb to the effect that "the stops, as well as the steps, of a good man are ordered of the Lord."

II

When you look at the next two words in the text, however, you begin to raise your eyebrows a bit. For Paul says not only that "all things work together" but that they work "for good."

Here you begin to call a halt. "Paul," you say, "wait a minute, old fellow. Let's be honest and not take too much for granted. I can't follow you that far. I'm willing to say that all things work together. But for good? Well, I don't know about that. Was it for good that this college boy had to give up his schooling to enter service? Was it for good that this little girl surrendered her life to polio last week? Was it for good that this husband was taken away, leaving a wife and five children to make their own way? I can't see that all things happen for the best."

"Don't misunderstand me," Paul comes back. "I did not claim that all things happen for the best. What I said was that all things can be made to work together for good. And I can see that if we are going to get anywhere together, we must talk a little more about this word 'good.'"

"All right," you say, "then shoot."

"Well," says Paul, "read on a little further. 'All things work together for good to them that love God, to them who are the called according to his purpose. For whom he did foreknow, he also did predestinate to be conformed to the image of his Son.' So, then, the good I am talking about is not necessarily something which is to your liking. It is rather something which is good for you; and the highest good anybody knows anything about is to grow into the likeness of the Son of God, to be conformed to his image."

You had not thought about it in that way, and so you begin to sit up and take notice.

"Well," you say, "that's a horse of another color."

"Yes," says Paul, "I know what's in your mind. You are wondering why it is that, if God is good and if he governs this world by his providential care, so many bad things happen. The reason is this: We live in two worlds at the same time.

We live in the world of the spirit, but we also live in the physical world with our bodies. This physical world is subject to natural laws, and God does not exempt us from the laws of this natural order. We say we are in a Father's keeping, and yet nature is impartial. The sun shines on the evil as well as on the good. A drought will bring suffering on both. An accident will remove the useful as well as the useless. A clot in the artery will prove fatal for a saint as well as for a sinner."

"Well," you say, "what's going on here? I seem to have lost my Providence Road. Where's the sense in that sort of business?"

"Right here," says Paul. "Can't you see that once you and God get together on what life is all about, that it is not to have a good time but to become a good person—good in the sense that it is heading toward Christ, toward his likeness— then all these things you call 'bad' can be turned into profit? You know that the secret of success in business is to be able to capitalize on your liabilities—like those men who made a bar of soap and were sick because it was so light, and then decided to tell the world that it floats. Use a little imagination, man. Don't you remember that lady who fell and broke her hip? While she was in the hospital flat on her back she had to look up, and when she looked up she saw God, and she's been a different person ever since. Don't you remember that singer whose friend said about him, 'If only something could happen to break his heart, he would have the greatest voice in Europe'?"

And while the Apostle talks, something happens to you. Your mind begins to stretch a notch or two. You grow up from a child, in whose world everything works out to your liking, or you sulk. You become now an adult. You see that, just as you cannot save your child from his spills if he is going to learn to ride his bicycle, neither can you expect God to have things always to your liking if you are going to learn to find the highest good. While you grow you are not without your

79

growing pains; yet you find a new peace of mind, because you know that even if the worst happens it can be turned into the best. And at that point you get back on Providence Road.

III

Yet there is one more question you have about this matter: How can I be sure this Providence Road will ever get where it is going?

God says it will, doesn't he? Listen: "My counsel shall stand . . . ; I have purposed it, I will also do it."

"Yes," you say, "but what about this business of free will? You say that we have a right of choice. Well, take me, for instance. If I have a free will, can't I turn off Providence Road at Oxford Place? In that case I'll never get to Providence Church. Or take this whole, wide world. If God thinks he's ever going to get a homecoming with dinner on the grounds at Providence Church, when communism is still running loose in this world, he's got another think coming."

Well, let's see. Free will is a fact, and yet we know there are limits upon freedom. For example, a friend of mine has a beautiful little cocker spaniel which he prizes highly. He cannot let him run loose because the automobiles might run over him, and he doesn't want to keep him shut up in a box. So he put a collar on his dog and tied a chain to it. On the other end was a metal ring slipped over a wire some forty feet long, with the ends of it fastened to two trees. The dog is free to play on both sides of the wire, and can run up and down one end of it to the other. He is free, and yet his freedom is limited.

Or look at this picture. I sat down once to play checkers with an expert. We played one game after another, with the same result—he always won. When we started a new game, he never knew how I was going to move. There were many different moves on the board, and I was free to make the ones I chose. Yet by the time we had played a while he knew that, though he could not predict my plan of campaign, he could predict the outcome. He knew he would win. "I have purposed," says God, "and I will do it."

And then here is another fact that is true, when you stop to think about it: it is possible to guide free persons from above their freedom, without interfering with it.

This is something businessmen do all the time. The whole advertising business is based on it. You cannot override the freedom of your customer and force him to buy the car you are selling. But you can show him a picture of it in a magazine and on a billboard, and you can keep telling him on radio and television that it is just the car he needs. When he comes in to buy, it is in line with your plan, and yet he acts of his own free will and accord.

That is something parents know about too. When your child turns the corner of adolescence and begins to assert his own independence, his own freedom, then you have to shift gears. You change from the first gear of direct command to the second gear of indirect suggestion. One father said that when he had a book he wanted his fifteen-year-old son to read he wouldn't think of asking him to read it. He just put it on the table by a comfortable chair and left it—and it was read. A mother who was troubled because her son away at college would not write home told her brother that it had been three weeks since she had had a line, yet she had written nearly every day begging him to answer. The brother made a small wager that he could get an answer in less than a week. He wrote just a note, put a postscript at the bottom saying, "In case you are running short on cash I am enclosing a ten-dollar bill," and then conveniently forgot the enclosure. He had an answer in the next mail. "Dear Uncle Willie: About that ten dollars, etc."

Once we see the possibility of such guidance from above, the door is open to faith in providence. All such acts of personal power as we have described are imperfect, but they help us to imagine a higher control on the part of God, preserving our freedom, and using free men for higher purposes than their own.

There is mystery in this matter of providence, without a doubt; and yet to deny the truth of it does not get rid of the mystery. Two choices open before you: either you can believe in fate, according to which we are going it blind; or you can believe that there is a Wisdom wiser than our own, which is working with us for our good. As for me, I choose the latter; and I am sure that as long as God is able to make the wrath of men to praise him, Providence Road will reach its journey's end.

The Holiness of God

"Holy, holy, holy is the Lord of hosts."
—ISAIAH 6:3

You must have noticed how some people who appear dull and unresponsive on the surface turn out, on further acquaintance, to be full of interest and altogether most worth-while companions. So it is with certain ideas. Few people who saw in the paper an announcement of a sermon on the holiness of God would be drawn to church to hear it. But though the idea seems as colorless as a laundry list, it turns out to be as contemporary as this morning's sunrise and as interesting as the *Reader's Digest*.

Take it, for example, from the point of view of the history of the word "holy." It has been said that every word has a romance behind it. Certainly that is true concerning this word. When first it was used, it carried nothing more than the idea of separateness. My right hand, for example, is holy with respect to my left hand.

Then as time went on the meaning grew to cover not simply the fact of separation but the cause. Why is God different from men? Men looked about them and saw lightning strike and heard thunder roar and were filled with a sense of the power of God. So they said it was God's power that made him holy.

Only after many centuries was there given to prophets like Amos and Hosea and Isaiah the great revelation that the essence of holiness in God is moral excellence—that the

83

thing which makes God distinct from man, which makes him holy, is not the greatness of his power but the purity of his character. It seems passing strange to us that there ever could have been any other idea. God and goodness, God and rightness, God and morality—they are one and the same thing with us. But it was an amazing revelation when the prophets first proclaimed that God's holiness lies in his righteousness; and it revolutionized religion, transforming it from mere superstitious magic to the controlling principle in man's life.

Take a concordance some time and turn to the topic "the holy one of Israel," to see how often it appears in the pages of the Bible. That phrase stands out from the pages of the Book of life because its meaning is written large in the business of life. See now how that statement can be substantiated.

I

For one thing, the holiness of God sets the standard for our conduct. We talk about the "standard of living." A person's standard of living is high or low according to the kind of food and housing and clothing he has. Economically our standard of living is determined by material things. But morally our standard of living is determined by the quality of holiness in the character of God.

There is a manuscript of the Constitution of the United States so written that, when it is held at a distance, the shading of the letters looks like a picture of George Washington. In the Constitution is seen a character. The constitution of life is but a portrait of the character of God. It is called the moral law, and it finds its summary in the Ten Commandments. If we could take the Ten Commandments and so shade the letters as to make them show the face of God, we would have as nearly as it can be had a transcript of the quality of holiness in his character. There is something in holiness which says, "Do this," and something else which says, "Don't do that." The dividing line is the line which divides right from wrong. The character of God sets a standard of conduct. It commands what is right, and it condemns what is wrong.

So it is that religion has everything to do with morality. In the early days of the Old Testament a man's belief in God did not necessarily affect his way of living. He could feel he was on good terms with a holiness of power and still be a regular scoundrel. When the prophets rose to the insight that the essence of holiness is moral purity, they began to bear down on the sins of the people. The theme song of Amos is that a morally holy God demands moral holiness in his people. They supposed they could go on sinning against one another and still be right with God, just so they went to the temple and offered their sacrifice. But the prophet minces no words in telling them they must put an end to selling the poor for a pair of shoes and accepting bribes in a court of justice. "Seek good, and not evil, that ye may live," he says, "and so the Lord, the God of hosts, shall be with you."

The holiness of God still places its demands upon us. Religion is the touchstone of morality. Bible reading and church-going are not whitewash for wrongdoing. The guiding rule in every choice is not "Is it expedient?" or "Is it legal?" but "Is it right?" It may be legal to drink liquor, but is it right? It may be legal, to get a divorce on some flimsy excuse, but is it right?

You see, this question of the holiness of God is quite contemporary. It says that you cannot honor the cross on Sunday and practice the double-cross on Monday. It says with the psalmist that the man who has a right to stand with a clear conscience in the presence of God is not necessarily the man who goes to church or reads his Bible or says his prayers; it is the man who has "clean hands, and a pure heart." It says that matters are not safe for us, even though we sit in one of the high seats of the synagogue, unless we set the clock of our conduct by the character of our God.

II

There is a second meaning in our truth which is possibly less obvious than the first. The moral holiness of God makes him forever the enemy of sin. Sin is the very opposite of that moral goodness which is the essence of his character and the governing purpose in his creation. It makes straight for the defeat of his holy desire. He is bound, therefore, to be against it. The self-consistency of his character demands it. Inasmuch as he is God, inasmuch as he sits on the throne, and inasmuch as he has the upper hand over things in this world, sin is going to be the loser.

Now look at that fact as it works itself out in individual experience. It says that you can never sin and get away with it. It says that the man who sets out to do something wrong is whipped before he starts. It says that the holy God, who demands holiness in his people, has fashioned this world so that it pays to be good and it costs to do wrong. Any man who tries to beat that law is a fool. Do you think you are clever enough to outwit God? Do you think you can put one over on the Almighty? Look around you and see if you know anybody who has ever flown in the face of the commandments and not had to pay. The Good Book says that "the way of the transgressors is hard." It is written in the Book because it is written in life. Can you put your hand in the fire and not get it burned? When it comes to sin, our God is a consuming fire. Oh, my brethren, why are we such fools? Why do we keep on trying to get by with things we know are wrong when the cards are stacked against us?

But while the holiness of God speaks a word of warning against sin in the individual life, it stands as a strong source of confidence in the ultimate victory of right in the cosmic life.

In days like these it is natural that we should be concerned over the fate of our world. Will those who fight on the side of right win? Or will they go down before the onslaughts of evil? We sometimes wonder when we see a gangster take the wheel of his military machine and come near to driving it like a juggernaut over all opposition in one mighty blitzkreig. Have we then no hope for our world?

We have indeed—right here in this mighty fact of the holiness of God. A man was brought into court one day charged with running a gambling device known as a slot machine. The man chose to defend himself. When the prosecutor had presented his case, the defendant's turn came. "Judge," he said, "I am charged with conducting a gambling device. Will you tell me what gambling is?"

"Gambling," said the judge, "is risking something of value on an event the outcome of which is uncertain."

"Well, Judge," said the defendant, "according to your definition, I am not guilty. When a man puts a coin in this machine, the outcome of that event is not in the least uncertain. The inside mechanism is so adjusted that he cannot win. The thing is set against him. He is bound to lose."

And the man won his case!

So, it seems to me, is the contest in the large between good and evil. There is no gamble to it. The final outcome of this struggle is not in the least uncertain. If the holiness of God makes sin in the individual suicide, then that same holiness makes evil in the cosmic life self-defeating. God made this machine which we call the universe, and it was his privilege as its maker to set the works so that it would pay off in his favor. Inasmuch as his name is the Holy One of Israel, his favor is on the side of right, and when you sin you are going to lose, whether your name be Henry or whether it be Hitler.

III

There is a further meaning in our truth. The holiness of God guarantees that we can trust him and not be disappointed. The same self-consistency in the character of God which makes for inflexible certainty in the judgment of sin makes sure his trustworthiness in all other matters. He keeps his word about punishing sin, and he will keep any other word he gives. The holiness of God is our surety that we can depend on him.

Dependability seems such a rare trait in human nature. You leave your car at the garage, and the service manager tells you he will have it ready by four o'clock, but when you go for it you have to wait until five. You go out to hire a cook, and she promises to be on hand in the morning in time to get breakfast, but you never see her again. You have so many experiences with people who cannot be depended on you begin to wonder if there is any such thing as dependability.

There is, my friends. If you have failed to find it in people, you can always find it in God. If he says he will do a certain thing, he will do it. If he tells you he will take over your fears and anxieties and worries and give you peace of mind, he will do it if you trust him. If he tells you that though your sins be red like crimson he will still forgive, he will do it if you trust him. If he tells you that he will give you strength to do a difficult task, he will do it if you trust him. If he tells you that his grace is sufficient and he will see you through no matter what your need, he will do it if you trust him.

Once when David Livingstone's life was in danger from certain savages in Africa he grew frightened. But just for a moment. For then he reached into his pocket and took out his New Testament and read there the promise of a presence that would be with him always. He closed the book and put it back into his pocket and then said to himself: "It is the word of a gentleman of the most strict and sacred honor. . . . I feel quite calm now, thank God."

The words of a gentleman of the most strict and sacred honor! Any word of God is just that because it is backed by an ever-standing, never-changing holiness which says, "You can trust God, for he is trustworthy!"

XII

The Triumphant God

"And when they were come to the place, which is called
Calvary, there they crucified him."   —LUKE 23:33

Everybody seemed to know that something big was about
to happen. The atmosphere was electric. Yesterday he was in
Bethany. Last night they made him a supper there. The
village was crowded with Passover pilgrims from the up-
country of Galilee on their way to the feast in the Holy City.

For three years this Man—this Man who seemed to be
more than man—had been going up and down the country
talking to folks about God. The people liked him, but they
sensed the fact that lines were drawn between him and the
leaders in the city. They knew a crisis would surely come,
should he show his face during the feast, and they wondered
about his taking the chance. "Think you, will he come? Dare
he come? Will there not be trouble if he comes?"

Even as they questioned, word came he was on the way.
He was even now as close as Bethany. Tomorrow he would
enter the city. As crowded as the place was, the word spread
quickly. Next day a teeming throng streamed out of the city
to meet him.

His men had found a colt for him to ride, and other pilgrims had fallen in behind him. There were thus two proces-
sions moving toward each other; and somewhere between
Jerusalem and Bethany the crowds coming from the city met
the crowds coming to the city, and their enthusiasm caught

fire. They were so carried away that they took off their coats and spread them over the road, Sir Walter Raleigh fashion. They broke off branches from the palms which lined the roadside and laid them before him. Then, as with a trumpet, they gave him their salute: "Hosanna; Blesssed is he that cometh in the name of the Lord!"

I

Triumphal entry! So we call it, yet how hollow it must have sounded in his ears!

Here it is early Friday morning, and look at them now. He has been arrested in the garden, given a mock trial before the Sanhedrin, and stands before Pilate. Pilate wants to give him the benefit of the doubt. He remembers the custom of releasing a prisoner at the feast. He finds a notorious rebel, an acknowledged murderer named Barabbas, thinking surely the people will prefer the man named Jesus to such a criminal.

"Whom will ye that I release unto you? Barabbas, or Jesus?" he shouts to them.

"Barabbas! Barabbas! Give us Barabbas!" shout back the same crowds which spread palms before Jesus five days ago.

The governor is dumbfounded. Maybe they have misunderstood. He will give them one more chance to save an innocent man.

"What shall I do then with Jesus which is called Christ?" he calls out.

"Crucify him, crucify him!" is the incredible cry.

The details are attended to quickly. Luke gives the sequel simply: "And when they were come to the place, which is called Calvary, there they crucified him."

Triumphal entry indeed! To take a king and put him on a cross! How empty the praise, how hollow the shouts of the procession, how like a mockery the waving branches! What is there of triumph in being nailed to death like a criminal on a piece of wood? What do you imagine the members of that crowd thought of themselves when they got home and had time to remember what they had done? What would you think of yourself if on Sunday you gave him your hosannas and by Friday had been maneuvered into crying for his crucifixion? Triumphal entry indeed! Strange, is it not, that we still call it that?

And yet it is not so strange after all. For in a way beyond all their reckoning, above all their imagining, that crowd of palm-wavers was ushering the King on to his day of triumph. It was not the kind of triumph they expected. They thought he would be another David, who would set up his throne and with a supernatural power put down the enemies of Israel and bring the millenium for them. No, it was not the kind of triumph they expected. It was a new kind, God's kind. It was the triumph of the Cross. "And when they were come to the place, which is called Calvary, there they crucified him." See now this triumphant God at work.

II

At the place which is called Calvary the will of man ran counter to the will of God, and the result was a cross. Look at it for a moment—those two wood beams, one of them standing upright in the earth and the other nailed across it. Let that upright beam stand for the will of God, and the horizontal beam for the will of men. What it comes to is this: whenever the will of man runs counter to the will of God, the result is a cross.

That is what you are looking at when you see what happened there that day. Here was a Man whose life was on the beam of the will of God, but he was too good for them. The white light of his life showed up the dark places in their own: the blindness of Pharisees who could not see that God works by love more than by law; the greed of Sadducees who wanted to hang on to their monoply of a rake-off on temple graft; the political opportunism of Pilate with his backbone made out of spaghetti; the emotionalism of the crowd which could be swayed by propaganda; the weak-kneed loyalty of disciples who ran to cover when their leader was arrested. This kind of thing is not what God wills; and when it gets crossed with his will as you see it in Christ, then the result is always a cross. It happened then, and it still happens today.

You see it on a battlefield, where they put up little crosses, row on row. Whatever war is, it surely is not the desire of a God who named his Son the Prince of Peace. He wills that men shall live as brothers, and whenever their selfishness and greed send them marching across frontiers which are not their own, the result is a cross.

Sometimes you see it where it can't be seen, because it's carried on the inside. Here is a mother whose son becomes a wandering boy. The will of God for him is that he be clean and honest and kind. But he takes his fling in the far country, and the cross in her heart turns her hair white and puts lines in her face.

Or here is a husband. The will of God for him is that he be a faithful companion to his mate. But he spends all of his time working at his business to achieve a success that will bolster his self-esteem, and he has no time for his family. Then it happens that the wooden cross in the front door of his home is more than a decorative design.

Or here is a family of brothers and sisters, with their wives and husbands, come together to divide the property they have inherited. The will of God is that they be unselfish, kind, and generous. But someone wants more than his share, and the little gold cross on a chain which belonged to grandmother becomes more than a piece of jewelry.

Or here is a young man. The will of God is that his moral life be clean, that his dealings with the opposite sex be honest.

But he has a way of taking his fun where he can find it, with a thoughtless unconcern for the victims of his promiscuous amours.

There is a passage in Kierkegaard in which one such victim, brokenhearted, writes to her seducer: "John: I do not say 'My' John. That, I now see, you never were. I am heavily punished for ever letting such an idea be my joy. Yet—yet, mine you are—my seducer, my deceiver, my enemy, my murderer, the spring of my calamity, the grave of my joy, the abyss of my misery. I call you mine—and I am thine—thy curse forever. Oh, do not think I will put a dagger into you and slay you. But flee where you will, I am yours to the earth's ends, yours. Love a hundred others, but I am yours. I am yours in your last hour. I am yours, yours, yours—your curse." [1]

There was a cross there—for her and for him too—and it is a picture of what we are looking at now. Whenever the will of man runs counter to the will of God—on the battlefield or in business, in the home or in the community—the result is a cross like that one which stood on the place called Calvary.

III

Yet, while you stand looking at that cross, you see a strange thing happen. As far as the world could tell, it looked like the defeat of God. When the last nail was driven in, you could see old Annas and Caiaphas turning around to walk away, dusting their hands off and adjusting their cloaks about them and muttering to themselves, "Well, that's that. We'll call it a day and go on home. We'll not be troubled by this young upstart anymore. His sun has set. He's done for now." But they soon discovered their mistake. God took the very defeat they handed him and made it a triumph. Christ crucified has

[1] From *Entweider-Oder.*

become the power of God, the power by which he will finally win the world to himself.

I have never been able to explain the mystery of the Cross, how God turns tragedy into triumph. But I can report what I see, and what I see is this: The will of man running counter to the will of God always sets up a cross; yet that very cross, by the manner in which it is borne, has been the means of uncrossing those wills and setting them in harmony once again.

There was a popular monk in the Middle Ages who announced that he would preach one day on the love of God. On the day appointed the cathedral was filled with eager listeners. He waited till the setting sun caught the stained glass windows, flooding the place with its lovely coloring. Then when the last bit of light had faded from the windows he went to a golden candelabra, took a lighted candle, and walked to a statue of Christ hanging on the cross. He held the candle beside the wounded hands, then the wounded feet, then the open side, and finally the brow which had worn the crown of thorns. The great assemblage, deeply moved, sat still. They had come to hear a sermon on the love of God. They did not find what they had expected, but far more. They saw for themselves the love that bears wrong, and bears it in such a manner that it bears it away. It was something they would never forget.

When you come face to face with the cross, and take in something of its meaning, you can never forget it. It does something to you. You take off your hat, and get down on your knees, for you know you are on holy ground—ground made holy by a love that bears in order to bear away.

Jerome, who in the fifth century translated the Bible from Hebrew and Greek into Latin, spent the last years of his life in Bethlehem. Each day he looked upon the place of the Nativity and thought of the one who came to birth there.

"Every time I see the place where the Saviour was born," he says, "my heart enters into communion with the Infant Jesus. I say, 'O Lord Jesus, what a hard way you have chosen to bring me happiness. What shall I render you?' I hear the Child answer me, 'I do not ask anything but you.' I continue, 'Dear Child, I must give you something. I want to give you all my money.' But he answers me, 'Do not heaven and earth belong to me? Silver and gold are mine; I have need of nothing. Give your money to those who are in misery and I shall accept it as if it were given to me.' I say, 'I will do it but I wish also to give something to you. Otherwise I shall be dreadfully unhappy.' And I hear this sublime reply, 'If you wish to be so generous, I will tell you what you can give me. Give me your sin, your bad conscience, and the evil that weighs upon you.' I ask him, 'What do you want to do with it?' The Child answers me, 'I wish to lay it on my shoulders. That will be my great work and obligation. I want to carry your sins.'"

Stanley Jones tells about a man in India who found it so. He had a beautiful and intelligent wife, and he was faithful to her until he went to Europe on a business trip. There he took his first misstep, and continued his infidelity after he returned to India. The innocence and trust of his wife stabbed him like a knife. Finally came the crisis when he knew he would have to tell her. He dreaded it. He was afraid that her anger would wither him and that she would leave him. He told her the whole shameful story.

"I can never forget," he said, "the look of anguish that came over her face as the meaning of what I had done dawned upon her. She turned pale and, clutching at the pain in her heart, she sank upon the bed. I could see my sin torturing her. Then she rose and I expected the storm to break upon me, but instead she said, 'I love you still and I will not leave you.' Then," he said, "I saw in the anguished love of my wife the meaning of the cross. From her love I stepped up to the cross. I was a redeemed man from that hour."

When your will runs counter to the will of God, the result is a cross. But when love takes hold, it has a mysterious power to uncross those wills and set them in harmony once again—in the triumph of the cross.

"And I, if I be lifted up, will draw all men unto me."

"I was a redeemed man from that hour!"

"All men—unto me!"

XIII

The Saving God

"And Jesus said unto him, This day is salvation come to this house."   —LUKE 19:9

The Bible is a book about salvation, and the God of the Bible is a saving God. "I am the Lord thy God, the Holy One of Israel, thy Saviour." Thus the divine voice spoke to Isaiah. All the way from the Red Sea, where the Lord "saved Israel that day," to the last book in the Bible, where we see a multitude with robes washed "white in the blood of the Lamb," God is busy at the business of saving people.

The honest truth, however, is that few of us who call ourselves Christians know much about what it means to be saved. Often we preachers are to blame. We dress it out in words like "justification," "sanctification," "glorification," and offer it as a neatly wrapped package, bound in a technical cord and tied with a theological knot. Even if you succeed in getting the knot untied, you discover the contents are about as workable and meaningful for life as a Chinese puzzle. Yet you cannot escape the conviction that if we could forget the trappings for a while, if we could get back to the heart of it as we find it in the New Testament, if we could see it in all the beauty and simplicity and power it has in the hands of Jesus, then most of us would find ourselves crying out, "Lord, here am I. Save me!" Let us look, therefore, at the saving God at work.

I

The first thing we see is that God saves us right now. Of course it will last tomorrow, and the next day, and will run on out into the long future when we have no need of calendars. But salvation begins now.

Recall the story that surrounds our text. Jesus is on his way to Jerusalem and stops off at Jericho. A man named Zacchaeus lives there. Zacchaeus is not too well liked in his home town because he is a publican—which means he collects taxes for the alien Romans. He has heard that this man Jesus' friendliness does not stop even at publicans, and he wants to see him. The other people want to see Jesus too, and the street is crowded. Everybody takes a special delight in elbowing this public enemy number one to the rear. Being too short to see over their heads, Zacchaeus runs on down the street and climbs into a low-limbed sycamore tree to await the procession. When Jesus comes alongside, he notes the eager interest of this tree-sitter and invites himself home with him. Zacchaeus is overjoyed. He comes sliding down so fast that, as legend has it, he knocks some bark off the tree—with the result that you will see white splotches on the trunk of a sycamore tree to this day.

After they reach the house and talk for a while, something happens inside Zacchaeus. He begins to see things differently.

"Lord," he says to Jesus, "I am willing to share up to half of all I have with the poor. If I have cheated anybody by overcharging him on his taxes, I will give him back four times as much."

"This day is salvation come to this house," Jesus replies.

This day—this very hour—salvation has come. It is a present thing, in the hands of the saving God. Yet how many Christians do you know who expect any present benefit from being saved?

"I am a sick man," a patient said to a doctor friend of mine, "and I am going to fall to sleep pretty soon. But I am a Christian. I know I am *going to be saved*."

Going to be saved! Going to be freed from punishment in the life to come! Of course that is a part of it, and a blessed part. But it is only a part. This is not an ordinary life insurance policy, which pays only at the policyholder's death. It is endowment insurance, collectible even before age sixty-five. You can clip your coupons now.

Here is a doctor who has worked for years in clinics for people troubled in body and soul, and he says these astonishing words: "Most Christians do not expect their religion to do them any great or immediate good."

How like we are to the old woman trudging along the road with a heavy pack on her back! A man in a wagon offered her a lift, and she climbed in, but sat there still holding her pack on her back. When he suggested that she put it in the back of the wagon, she replied, "Oh, but it is so kind of you to carry me, I don't want to make you carry my burden too. I'll carry that."

We smile at the old lady, and yet we do just as she did. We believe God can save our souls sometime in the future. As for the present—why, we shall have to manage for that. But God refuses to be put off. "This day," he says.

II

But what does it mean to be saved right now? If you want it in a definition, here it is: It means the removal of dangers menacing to life and the consequent placing of life in conditions favorable to its free and healthy expansion. But if you want it in a demonstration—as you probably do—you can find it in the lives of those who have been here when it happened to them.

Look at Zacchaeus, for example. According to our definition, there are two parts in being saved. God saves us *from* whatever is damaging to life; he saves us *to* whatever makes for its free and healthy expansion. The thing Zacchaeus was saved *from* was an itching palm, a covetous spirit, a love of money. He was so much taken with chasing the shekel that he was willing to be called a publican and to be bracketed by his townspeople with sinners. Moreover his craving for riches had made him steal—he confessed himself a thief when he told Jesus that if he had cheated anybody he would give back four times as much, for fourfold repayment was what the law demanded of a thief. To be money-minded like that is to be in danger. Look at King Midas. Love of gold leads to a heart of gold—a heart that is yellow and hard. Zacchaeus was headed full-speed ahead in that direction. But he was saved—saved from love of money. At the same time he was saved *to* something—saved to love of men, saved to a true standard of values, saved to a spirit of sharing that made him willing to give half his fortune to the poor. Even we dollar-mad Americans see the difference in the man and applaud it. Jesus calls that "salvation."

Wherever you walk up and down in the Gospels, you find that same thing taking place. George Matheson has a beautiful book called *The Representative Men of the New Testament*. The thread which runs throughout is the truth that every person who went into the building of the New Testament required two portraits—one before, the other after, he was saved. They were saved from what they had been before, saved to what they became afterward. They were so different that it takes two pictures to portray them.

Look at Paul. Better still, bring him in and ask him.

"Paul," we say, "what can you tell us out of your own experience about what it means to be saved?"

The face of that little crippled traveler glows, for he would rather do such a thing than eat.

"When I first started out," he says, "I was all mixed up in my mind. I saw God all wrong. I still lived in the Old Testament. I thought that the Jews had a monopoly on God, and that religion was obeying rules, and that Jesus was an impostor. Then I was saved—saved from the error in my beliefs, saved to the truth about God. That truth has set me free, and the one thing I'm out for now is to spread that truth."

Turn to Peter and ask him the same question.

"At first," he answers, "I was weak in my will, weak as water. I didn't have the courage of my convictions. I let a little maid in the high priest's court make me tell a lie about my Lord. Then I was saved. Now I am able to stand up before the chief of police in Jerusalem and tell him that all his jails can't scare me off from preaching my gospel."

When these two men were saved, they became such different men that they had to have different names. Contrast with them the people today who make salvation a technicality, who count themselves saved because "the great transaction's done" but show no before-and-after difference. One would wish to say to such folks: "Saved from what? You are always anxious, vexed with little fears and apprehensions. When trouble comes, you are sure you cannot stand it. When tasks arise, you are certain you cannot perform them. When it is suggested that you surrender your pet self-indulgences—things like losing your temper and ruining people's reputations—you are convinced you haven't the strength. Saved from what? Not from fear, weakness, selfishness, temper. And if you say, Saved from hell—what is hell but the final subjugation of the soul to such sins as you are now cherishing?"

No, Jesus promises salvation from real and present evils: "Be not afraid." "Go, . . . sin no more." "Fear not, little flock." It is more than a status decreed by legal enactment. It is new life, liberation from old habits, anxieties, fears. It lifts horizons, overcomes impossibilities, and at the center of life sets the

101

stirring conviction that you can do what you ought to do. The heart of it is power for victorious living.

III

Of course there is one more question you are asking: "If God saves us right now, and if it means that he gives us power for victorious living, how can I get saved?"

For the answer to that question look at the passage of scripture which we usually recognize as the key to the whole New Testament: "God so loved the world, that he gave his only begotten Son, . . . that the world through him might be saved." The saving God saves us through Jesus Christ. You get saved when you get hold of Christ—or rather when Christ gets hold of you.

Look again at Zacchaeus. When was he saved? Salvation came to his house and to his heart when he welcomed Jesus into them.

In the First World War a soldier's face was horribly disfigured in battle. When he realized his condition, he was bitter and wished himself dead. One day a plastic surgeon examined him and promised to restore the disfigured face if he could be furnished a photograph to go by. But the soldier was too despondent to be impressed. Besides he had no photograph.

"It doesn't matter, Doc," he said. "I was never much to look at anyway. Suppose you just make me like that picture on the wall."

The picture happened to be a portrait of Christ; and, according to the story, the surgeon did take that for his model. One day all the bandages were removed, and the man was allowed to look in a mirror. He found himself gazing on a face strikingly different from his old one, and strikingly similar to the picture on the wall.

That night the man was too absorbed in thought to care for sleep. He was thinking of his new face and also of the picture on the wall. "Since I look like him," he decided, "there is but one thing to do—I must become like him." From that day forward he began to be kind to the nurses and attendants, to speak words of encouragement to the other patients. In time he did become genuinely like the one whose picture hung on the wall.

If your heart has been disfigured in the battle of life, know that the saving God can remold it after the likeness of his Son Jesus Christ. He offers you a salvation that will begin today and will save to the uttermost of your need—save from weakness and from worry, from cynicism and from sin, from temper and from timidity, from drink and from drudgery, from guilt and from greed, from hate and, finally, from hell—to a life of peace, and purity, and power. Climb down, then, and show hospitality to the Christ who passes by. Welcome him to your house and to your heart, that through him the saving God may save you this day and for evermore.

XIV

The Healing God

"For I am the Lord that healeth thee."
—EXODUS 15:26

Good health is something in which every one of us is interested. When you stop to think about it, you realize what a rare possession it is. Set out to engage a room in any hospital, and you discover at once how many people there are who are physically ill. Remember that many people never go to a hospital except as a last resort, and you can look beyond the number who have been hospitalized and see a vast multitude still sick at home. To that number add those who are mentally sick, and to that number those who are spiritually sick, and to that number those who are heartsick, and you have a total from which few of us are exempt.

In the light of that fact there is a verse in the Old Testament which fairly stands out on the page. The children of Israel have just crossed the Red Sea. They enter the wilderness of Shur, the tract of desert which separates Egypt from Palestine, and go three days' journey. At the end of some thirty-three miles they come to the well of Marah, a basin of some six or eight feet in diameter, with two feet of water in it. They are glad to see water after a long trip in the desert. But when they start to drink, the water turns out to be disagreeably bitter and salty. They turn on Moses, the leader who has brought them out from a settled home into a place of wandering. Moses calls upon God, and God shows him a tree. Moses takes the tree and casts it into the basin, and the waters are made sweet.

Then the Lord sets up "a statute and an ordinance"—that is, he lays it down as a rule for their subsequent guidance—that in all their future difficulties he will be their helper and deliverer. If they will listen to his voice and do his commandments, he will put on them none of the diseases which they knew in Egypt. He will always act as their healer as he had just done at Marah. For, he says, "I am the Lord that healeth thee."

I

The first thing we see in this text is that in the struggle between ourselves and our illnesses God is on our side. In other words, disease is not the will of God for us. When you are sick, it will give a boost to your spirit to know that God wants you to get well. His will is your health of body and mind and spirit. When he spoke to Moses he said, "I am the Lord that healeth thee." And when he sent his Son, that Son spent so much of his time healing blind people and deaf people and lame people that folks call him the Great Physician. Disease is not the will of God; and when you and I get sick and struggle to get well, we have a right to tell ourselves that God is on our side and the great power of the universe is working with us.

Yet, having said that, we must come right back and say that physical health is not God's main desire for us. In one of the books in the Bible we read about a tree whose leaves are for the healing of the nations. That is a picture of the Christian faith. The main business of a fruit tree is not to grow leaves but to yield fruit. The main business of life under God is not to grow healthy bodies but Christian characters. So God permits disease as one of the conditions under which we can seek to grow in likeness to him and by means of which we can increase in the fruits of the Spirit. When we

105

look at sickness in the light of God, what we see is something like this: He wants us to get rid of all the disease we can. When we can't, he wants us to use it in the business—which is our main business—of growing fruit.

So then we come back to our text. We want to know whether God still exerts any healing power. Does our religion have anything to do with our health? Following the Red Sea the people of Israel would have gladly awarded to God a D.D. degree—he had proved himself their Deliverer from Danger. But here he is claiming an M.D.—"I am the Lord that healeth thee." What about that?

The answer is that the tree of Christian faith has not only fruit, but leaves as well, and the leaves are for healing. That is a fact which the main body of the Christian Church has sometimes forgotten. Because it has forgotten it, we have witnessed the growth of groups which claim the power to exercise healing by faith. The amazing growth of some sects, for example, can be explained only by the fact that their leaders hit upon an element in the Christian faith which the regular churches have been neglecting. Yet the Lord that healeth is our God as well, and we cheat ourselves when we do not seek the health he can give.

Of course God gives health in co-operation with physicians. Sometimes you meet people who think that if they are going to depend on God, they must leave the doctor out. Sherwood Eddy says that in his early life his eyes were weak and he needed something to help him read. At first he prayed that God would make his eyes strong and refused to go to see a doctor. But nothing happened. Later he saw how foolish he was and went to a doctor to get help. Some doctors are sensitive and get their feelings hurt when another physician is called in for consultation. But God is not so touchy as that. The doctors are ministers of God, to whom his healing truth has been revealed, and we do his will when we seek their help.

Yet your doctor would be the first to admit that without the help of God he would be helpless. He depends all together for his healing touch upon the great urge to health which God has implanted in this world. When he is called upon to check an infection or to perform an operation, he could get nowhere without the principle of healing which is there before he was called in. He can make the incision, and remove the cause of trouble, but he has no power to make the tissues knit again. That power comes from somewhere else. Without the help of the healing God, even our most skillful doctors would be helpless, and they would be the first to admit it.

II

We go on to note furthermore that our Christian faith can help us to health by giving us a healthy mind. Thoughts are things—real things—and an unhealthy thought is a germ which, if held onto long enough, will get down into your body and poison you so that you become physically ill. Mental conditions can upset your normal physical functions, can weaken your resistance to infection, and can actually cause physical changes in your vital organs.

Doctors at the Columbia-Presbyterian Medical Center in New York studied fifteen hundred patients suffering from a variety of illnesses and found that an emotional upset lay at the root of more than half the cases. At John Hopkins a doctor examined fifty patients who complained of nausea and could find a definite organic reason in only six cases. The rest were literally worrying themselves sick—like one man whose symptoms began the day he lost his job. A study of a hundred tubercular patients revealed that those who were emotionally disturbed had a swifter form of disease than those free of strain. One man found that his ulcer flared up every time his mother-in-law came for a visit.

After older doctors had failed to cure a little girl of persistent vomiting, a recent graduate of the Cornell Medical Center was consulted. The laboratory reported no organic difficulty. The young man knew something of the effect of mind on body, and so he sat down to have a friendly talk with her. He found she was suffering from a severe emotional upset. She had remarked in a moment of feeling that she wished her teacher would die. Three days later the teacher did die of heart failure. The child, who thought her wish had caused the tragedy, reacted with stomach trouble. When the doctor convinced her she was not responsible, she recovered.

Doctors are now saying that it is more important to know what sort of patient has the disease, than what sort of disease the patient has. That is where religion comes in, because it is the business of religious faith to make persons that are whole. I have on my shelf a book by Charles T. Holman titled *The Religion of a Healthy Mind*. Religion has everything to do with a healthy mind, because the doctors say that those mental states which cause most illness are resentments and hatred, anxieties and fears, and self-centeredness. A good dose of Christianity is what most of us need to get rid of these things which make us sick. The Bible has been saying that a long time, and we have paid little attention to it. Now that the doctors are saying the same thing we are more willing to listen. Look at this word from Dr. William Sadler: "If people lived in a truly Christian way, half the diseases would drop off tomorrow morning." And then listen to Dr. C. G. Jung, a world authority in nervous diseases: "Among all my patients thirty-five years and older there has not been one whose problem in the last resort was not that of finding a religious outlook on life."

A minister went to the Mayo Clinic, a sick man. He could not eat; he could not sleep; he had sledge-hammer pains in the back of his neck; he was horribly worried about the future. How long would he be able to carry on? Would it be necessary for him to resign from his work? When he was examined, it was discovered there was nothing organically wrong with him. His tissues were all healthy, and every organ in his body was as sound as a dollar. The specialist into whose hands he finally was put said to him, "As a clergyman I suppose you read the New Testament?"

"Yes," he answered.

"Well," said the doctor, "why in thunder don't you believe it? It says among other things, 'Be not anxious,' and you have been nothing but anxious. You have been worrying over your sermons, wondering how they would be received. You have been worrying over your position in the community, wondering how you would be received. You have made yourself sick through needless anxiety. Go home and stop worrying or even thinking about yourself, and for goodness sake put a little trust in the God whose minister you profess to be."

You see, it is the doctors who are preaching Christian faith to us now. They are telling us we can find the healing power of God by deliverance from those mental states which make us sick, and by filling our minds with the truth which has the power to give health. Pasture your cow on a field of spring onions and the milk that you drink will not taste like sweet clover. Pasture your mind on a field of disease-laden thinking and the body you get will be broken. Whether we like it or not, as a man thinketh, so is he. Wherefore, says Paul, whatsoever things are true and honest and just and pure and lovely and of good report, keep on thinking—pasture your mind— on these things.

III

Finally, we see that the healing power of God can be had by those of us whose illnesses come from being spiritually out of joint.

A young woman sought to justify her sex license by saying, "But it is all right if you can get away with it." If you can get away with it! That's the rub. You can't get away with it to save your life. God has written it down that right is right and wrong is wrong, and you can't do wrong and feel right about it. That feeling of wrongness is what we call guilt, and guilt is a germ that makes you sick. A doctor named Stanley Cobb studied hundreds of cases of arthritis and asthma and found that 68 per cent of the patients expressed feelings of guilt. The psalmist was a better man of medicine than he knew when he wrote, "There is no health in my bones because of my sin." (R.S.V.) When Jesus set out to cure the man sick of the palsy, the first thing he said to him was, "Thy sins be forgiven thee." It is not very far from a bad conscience to a sick body, and the only healing that man can find must come from the hand of the healing God.

Norman Vincent Peale tells in *The Art of Living*[1] about a man who went to a doctor with every symptom of serious illness. The physician examined him thoroughly and sent him away with the report that he was organically sound. But in two weeks the patient was back again.

"Doctor," he said, "I want you to examine me again, for I am really at my wits' end. I feel very bad. I am nervous and upset. I cannot eat or sleep, and I am completely miserable."

The physician repeated his examination and again could find no physical cause for illness.

"There is," he said finally, "as far as I can see, nothing definitely wrong with you physically. Your body is not functioning normally, to be sure, but I find no evidence of organic trouble." He paused and then continued, "You must have something on your conscience. Have you done anything that is wrong, that you are ashamed of?"

"I will not stand for being insulted by you," cried the

[1] Copyright 1937 by Norman Vincent Peale. Published by Garden City Books.

patient angrily. "I came here for medical advice, not a sermon."
And he stalked out.

Not long afterward he returned, in a much different spirit.

"Doctor," he said, "I will confess that you put your finger
on the truth of it. I have done something very wrong."

He went on to tell his story. He was managing his brother's
share of their father's estate while the brother lived abroad.
He had started keeping for himself part of the income due
his brother, knowing that he could arrange his records so
that no one would ever know. But his own conscience knew,
and the disease in it infected his whole body.

"How much can you pay your brother?" the doctor asked.
When the patient answered, he ordered, "Write the check."

Then they immediately composed a letter to the brother,
confessing the theft and promising to make regular payments
till all should be made up. They enclosed the check, sealed
the envelope, and walked together to the mail chute.

As the man dropped the letter into the chute, his face
showed that he had dropped the burden from his life.

"I never knew what the word 'relief' meant before," he said.

The physician, in recounting the story, said that the patient
when he came to him with this thing on his mind was actually
ill, but that to give him medicine or treat him in any other
than a spiritual way would, in his opinion, have been mal-
practice. The trouble with the man was that he had a sense
of guilt, which affected his entire organism.

When people get sick they usually begin praying. That
is a good sign. But if your prayer is to help you get well, it
must lead to obedience to the laws of health. That means that
sometimes it will send you to a doctor. Sometimes it will lead
to faith which conquers fear. And sometimes it will make you
say, "God be merciful to me a sinner." Thus will you find
health at the hands of the healing God.

XV

The God of All Comfort

"Blessed be God, even the Father of our Lord Jesus Christ, . . .
the God of all comfort." —II CORINTHIANS 1:3

Our text comes from Paul's second letter to the Corinthians.
Paul had founded the church at Corinth and then gone on
to his work in Ephesus. There he heard that things were not
going smoothly in the Corinthian church. Some people were
living immoral lives, and certain individuals who did not
agree with his ideas about the gospel were criticizing him and
causing factions in the church.

Now Paul's churches were Paul's children, and when any
of them were abused he suffered as a parent suffers when his
child is injured. In the paragraph which follows the text he
says, "Now I would like you to know about the distress which
befell me in Asia, brothers. I was crushed, crushed far beyond
what I could stand." (Moffatt.) The thing that was crushing
him was the trouble in the church. He took it to heart, and
it cut him to the quick. He was heartbroken—so much so,
he says, that "I despaired even of life." (Moffatt.) If ever
anyone needed comfort that man was Paul.

So he sat down and wrote a letter, putting his critics in their
places, and pointing out how the love of Christ would correct
their irregularities of living and heal their divisions. He waited
anxiously to hear whether his letter had made matters better
or worse. Good news came; his anxiety was relieved; and so he
sat down to write again. The second letter to the church at

Corinth begins with this doxology: "Blessed be God, even the Father of our Lord Jesus Christ, the Father of mercies, and the God of all comfort; who comforteth us in all our tribulation."

I have rehearsed this bit of history which lies behind these words in order to suggest that Paul knows what he is talking about. He is not speaking from hearsay. He has been there, as we say. He was in trouble and God came to him with comfort, and so he has a right to speak to anyone who may be interested about the God of all comfort.

I

Our text assures us that the God whom Paul writes about is able and willing to comfort his people. But before we can appropriate this comfort we have to understand what Paul means when he uses the word. The word "comfort" has suffered at the hands of its friends. We think of it as a weak word. We think of a child who falls and bumps his head and comes crying to his mother, who takes him in her lap and wipes his eyes and soothes the hurt. We confuse the word "comfort" with the word "pity." To pity is to feel grief or pain over the misfortunes of others, with a desire to relieve. So we think of the comfort of God as the pity of God. We suppose that means he is a "wiper of eyes." And there is nothing in that idea to challenge the hero in our souls. It is safe to assume that someone, when he noticed that this sermon has to do with "The God of All Comfort," said to himself: "Too bad! I'm not interested in a God who does nothing but cuddle and coddle. Why do the preachers always make religion a thing for cry-babies? Why don't they put some iron in it once in a while and make it appeal to a man who has some manhood about him?"

All I have to say to that sentiment is: "Amen, brother! The very thing you are asking for is the very thing this text is talking about." "Comfort" is not a weak word. It is just about as strong as any word you can find. Notice, if you will, that the last four letters in this word are the first four letters in the word "fortitude." Now fortitude is not weak. It means strength of mind to meet or endure pain or peril. In the older versions of the Bible "comfort" was used interchangeably with "strengthen." In the Wycliffe Bible of 1382 the words about the boy Jesus which read in our version, "and the child waxed and was comforted," are given. You see more clearly when you break down the word. *Com* means "with," and *fortis* means "strong." To be comforted is to be strengthened by "being with." The comfort of God is the strength which comes from being with God.

Joseph Conrad in one of his essays quotes from a letter from Sir Robert Stopford. Stopford was one of Nelson's men. He was commander of one of the ships with which Nelson chased to the West Indies a fleet nearly twice as large. Describing the hardships and experiences of that desperate adventure, Stopford wrote the words: "We are half-starved, and otherwise inconvenienced by being so long out of port. But our reward is—we are with Nelson."

Life so often brings us to the point where it asks the question, "Can you take it?" There are two sides to this business—the active and the passive, the doing and the enduring—and the second is by far the harder part. You can work night and day in some good cause and like it; but when you get sick and have to give up your work and lie there in bed, can you take it? You can live uprightly and scatter your good deeds like autumn leaves over the earth, but when someone criticizes you, as those scandalmongers in Corinth were criticizing Paul, can you take it?

"We are half-starved," said Stopford, "but we are with Nelson." That presence made a difference. That presence outweighed the peril. That presence enabled them to take it—because it made them strong, because it gave them comfort.

114

So, says Paul, God is the God of all comfort, not because he takes us in his lap and wipes the tears from our eyes and rocks us to sleep, but because he stands there pulling for us and saying, "I'm counting on you, old fellow, to take it like a man; and I'm here to help you by standing by you." We are up to our necks in trouble, but—we are with God!

II

Of course it is no easy matter to take trouble even though we know we have God standing by to help us. As a matter of fact, so far from looking for help from God, we are more likely to curse God for our unhappy lot. We suppose that if God had been on the job we would never have got in such a fix, and we blame him for his negligence. But such rebellion is a blind alley, as we learn sooner or later. It is a red-letter day for us when we listen to Paul long enough to have him tell us the whole story about trouble.

We can do more than take trouble, Paul says. We can get something out of it. We can turn adversity to advantage if we are willing to accept the help of the God of all comfort.

"We rejoice in our tribulations," Paul wrote to the Romans. That sounds foolish. When you understand what he means, though, you see he is talking sense. What he means is that we triumph in our trouble, knowing that trouble produces endurance, and endurance produces character. In other words, when trouble comes you can take it better if you see that out of it you can emerge a better person. Of course it would be foolish to go out of your way to ask for trouble just to have a chance to grow a little character. There is sound wisdom in the saying, "Never trouble trouble till trouble troubles you." But when, in the way of duty, you encounter trouble, it is a help to know that what seems a total loss can be turned into profit.

Take sickness, for example. One day I went to see a mother in the hospital. She had been there for weeks. "It is no fun lying here in bed," she said, "but I think I have learned to get something out of this experience. The doctor tells me I will never get well until I learn to be patient. Now I have never had any patience with my children, or my husband, or my friends. If in these weeks in the hospital God can teach me to be patient, I'll be a better wife and mother." The God of all comfort was at work there.

Or take trouble between husbands and wives. There is no more useful place in all the world to know this truth than in the marriage relation.

"We have been married ten years," a distressed woman told her minister, "and we have two children. Of course we have had our little fusses before, but they always blew over. Last week end, however, my husband told me he didn't love me any more. Yesterday when I asked if he still meant it he said he did. I have been wondering if I ought to leave him and go back home."

"When you married your husband," the minister said, "did you promise to live with him as long as he loved you?"

"No," she answered, seeing the point. "There was no such condition. The vow said as long as we both should live, for better, for worse."

The minister suggested that, although it was not a pleasant prospect, she might look on her situation as an opportunity to show that strength of character called fidelity to duty.

"I see my duty," she said as she rose to go, "and I'm going to do it."

The God of all comfort was at work there.

III

But Paul suggests another direction in which adversity can be made to count for advantage. "Blessed be . . . the God of all comfort," he says; "who comforteth us in all our tribulation, that we may be able to comfort them which are in any trouble."

Our trouble, Paul says, can be used not only for our own

advantage but for the sake of other folks as well. So he writes in another place in this letter: "I rather glory in my infirmities . . . for when I am weak"—weak because of handicaps, because of hindrances—"then am I strong"—strong in opportunity to be of help to someone else. To see what he means you have only to stop and realize that the people who can help you most are not those who have never known trouble. They are rather those who have had trouble in full measure and handled it magnificently, and so have inspired within you a new courage.

Back in 1866 a boy was born in southern England named Arthur Pearson. From birth his eyes were weak, and by the time he was forty-seven the last flicker of light faded.

The following summer the First World War broke out, and within a few weeks blind soldiers began to appear in the hospitals in London. One day Pearson was called by telephone to come at once to a hospital. The doctors had told a young soldier that his sight was permanently destroyed, and he had gone into hysterics. Being unable to quiet him, they summoned Pearson with the hope that he—another man who had lost his sight—might be able to help the man.

The visit to the hospital revealed to Pearson a new life-work. He would organize a new hospital for blind soldiers. During the succeeding months he carried out his plan, founding St. Dunstan's Hospital, whose business is to help men and women blinded in war service to adjust to their new circumstance and find new hope and a fresh start. When the war ended he had no less than 1,700 blinded veterans under his care.

Pearson insisted that every man in the hospital learn Braille, that every man learn a trade that would make him self-supporting, and that every man co-operate to make St. Dunstan's the most cheerful place in all England. Whenever any patient lost his courage and self-control, and began to talk wildly of suicide, Pearson would visit the man, take his hand, and say quietly to him, "Old fellow, you know I'm blind too."

No one will ever know how many men Pearson saved from death or insanity, or how profoundly he altered the future in countless homes. When he died in 1921 all England rose to do him honor.

Since that time another war has come and gone, and other soldiers have come home blinded. And there stands St. Dunstan's, the lengthened shadow of Arthur Pearson, a friend to man. I imagine that, if Pearson had his life to live over again and were given the choice of sight or blindness, he would hesitate a long time before he decided against the way things actually turned out. In his very weakness he found the chance to be a strong tower.

That same chance belongs to everyone who faces trouble. You may not be able to found a St. Dunstan's, but by your brave handling of some difficult situation you can inspire courage and hope for other folks.

Several years ago one of our fine boys from the church went down in his ship. When the news reached his mother, she showed a magnificent fortitude. One of her friends asked how she kept from going to pieces, and this is what she said:

"What is our religion for, if not to make us strong?"

XVI

The God of All Grace

"And the God of all grace . . . shall himself perfect, establish,
strengthen you."   —I PETER 5:10 (A.S.V.)

The word "grace" is one of the jewels of our language. Take
it into your hand and look at it and its various meanings flash
like the brilliance of a many-faceted diamond. We speak of
saying grace at the table, which is our glad expression of
thanksgiving. We speak of a certain person as being a
gracious hostess, meaning that she possesses that delightful
quality called charm, which is a capacity for giving pleasure.
We say of a dancer that he is graceful, describing the harmony and symmetry of movement. We speak of a month
of grace allowed by an insurance company for the payment
of a premium after the passing of the due date—a practice
which most of us genuinely appreciate. The word "grace" in
its meanings is indeed as precious as a precious stone.

It will come not as a surprise, then—for those of us who
know him as he is—to discover that our text links the word
"grace" with the word "God." It speaks of him as "the God of
all grace." That means two things.

It means first that there is a certain attractiveness in the
way God deals with people. Our Lord Jesus Christ is the
picture of God in human dress, and the record describes him
in more than one place as being full of grace. One incident

119

will suffice. Recall the day he met the woman at the well and pointed out her sin. Instead of saying brutally, "Woman, you are an adulteress," he said graciously, "Go, call thy husband, and come hither." How delicately gracious that was! He never blinked the truth, but he handled the truth attractively. He was full of grace.

Second, when you speak of "the God of all grace," you mean not only attractiveness but kindness as well. You suggest the favor of God as the author and giver of all things, especially all good things. By grace we possess the gift of life. By grace we are surrounded by all the good things of life. And by grace we possess the good will of God. The word "grace" combines these two truths: attractiveness and kindness.

But in the New Testament the word "grace" has a more limited meaning. It takes that general idea of favor or kindness, and it brings it to bear on one particular place of human need. Like a magnifying glass which will gather up the rays of the sun and focus them on one point, so does the New Testament take hold of the great and gracious kindness of God and fix it upon the supreme need of us all—the need of a morally wrong person to become morally right. In short, the grace of God is the divine remedy which deals with the human disease called sin.

If you are not a sinner, then of course this grace will mean nothing to you. But if you ever have been disappointed in yourself, if you ever have been ashamed of yourself, if you ever have broken faith with yourself and fallen below your ideal, if you ever have looked on the life of Christ and been conscious of coming short—in a word, if you ever have stood in the shoes of the Philippian jailor and asked honestly, "What must I do to be saved?"—then the grace of God is the answer to your question.

Let us look now at the God of all grace at work and see what we can see.

I

The first thing we see is that God's grace is free. The sinner in need of grace needs nothing to recommend him except his need. You cannot work for the divine favor which sets a man right with God. You cannot buy it, and if you get it your money is no good when it comes to paying for it. Other things may come C.O.D., but not grace; it is free of charge. If ever a man gets to God, and finds what we call salvation, it is because God first of all has come to meet that man. Grace is free. It is kindness bestowed on one who has not deserved. It is even more gracious than that. It is kindness bestowed on one who ill deserves. It is infinite favor to the infinitely ill-deserving.

Have you heard the story about Bradley? Bradley was a little boy, and one morning he came down to breakfast and put on his mother's plate a piece of paper neatly folded. His mother opened it. She could hardly believe it, but this is what Bradley had written: "Mother owes Bradley: for running errands, 25 cents; for being good, 10 cents; for taking music lessons, 15 cents; extras, 5 cents; total, 55 cents." His mother smiled but did not say anything. When lunchtime came she placed the bill on Bradley's plate with the fifty-five cents. Bradley's eyes danced when he saw the money, and he thought his business ability had been quickly rewarded. But with the money there was another bill, which read: "Bradley owes Mother: for being good, 00; for nursing him through his long illness with scarlet fever, 00; for all his meals and his beautiful room, 00." Bradley's eyes then filled with tears. He put his arms around his mother's neck, and his little hand with the fifty-five cents in hers. "Take the money all back, Mama," he said, "and let me love you and do things for nothing."

That is grace. It loves us and does things for nothing. "While we were yet sinners, Christ died for us."

II

This grace which is the free favor of God, which bestows on us kindness that is undeserved, operates in two ways. For one thing, it cancels our indebtedness. It writes off our account as settled in full.

Sometimes you read of a church holding a ceremony for the burning of its note. For years there has been a debt on the building. That debt is in the form of a note held by a bank. All the members work hard and give their money and pay the debt. When it is paid, they all get together, and some man strikes a match to the note, and they all sing "Praise God from Whom All Blessings Flow." The mortgage is canceled, and the church is free of debt. That is what grace does. It burns the note. It cancels the mortgage. It puts us in the clear. The process by which grace does that is called pardon. It functions as forgiveness.

For example, Paul got off on the wrong foot. He was all wrong about God and salvation. He thought that Jesus was trying to "muscle in" on a business which was none of his business. Paul went to work to stamp out the doings of this upstart. He consented to the stoning of Stephen. He breathed out threatenings and slaughter against the Christians. One day when he was on his way to Damascus to arrest and imprison the Christians, Jesus met him and set him straight. Imagine how Paul's conscience must have hurt him. Imagine how his soul must have been eaten up with remorse. The sight of Stephen with the stones pounding his broken body—how it must have haunted Paul. But whatever of guilt there was on Paul's conscience Jesus cleansed away. Whether or not Jesus ever put it in these words, Paul knew that he was pardoned, and the debt was paid. The slate was clean. The past was as if it had never been. His sins would be remembered no more against him. Infinite favor to the infinitely ill-deserving!

Or think of Peter—that leader among men, the first to come out with the truth about Jesus, the one who had proclaimed his loyalty most loudly. Peter turned his back on his Lord. "I do not know the man," he said. Then Jesus looked at Peter, and in that look I think Peter saw not only disappointment, but pity and compassionate pardon; for it melted Peter into tears. I think Peter knew what that look meant: "Too bad that you would turn me down. But I can take it. I'll not hold it against you, old fellow. And whenever you think about it and your conscience hurts you for it, just remember that, so far as I am concerned, the past is as if it had never been." Infinite favor to the infinitely ill-deserving. The God of all grace at work at the business of forgiving sin!

God must enjoy the business of being God more when his grace is busy forgiving sinners than when he is doing all the many other things he has to do. During the First World War a story came out about a mother whose unusually brilliant son gave his life on the battlefront. He was a genius and had flowered early. From the first he had led his classes, and at Oxford he went on to win distinct honor. But he went to war, and his life was blotted out by an exploding shell. The mother dreamed a singular dream. She thought an angel came and told her she could have her son back for five minutes.

"Choose," said the angel, "what five minutes you will have. Will you have five minutes of his life when he was leading classes at Oxford? Or would you prefer to have five minutes of those days that he spent in the service of his country, those last days of his life?"

The mother thought for a moment.

"If I can have him back for five minutes," she said, "I should prefer to have him, not as an Oxford student, nor during his soldier days. If I can have him but five minutes, I want to have him as a little boy on a day he disobeyed me.

I remember how he ran into the garden, angry and rebellious. Then in a little while he came back and threw himself into my arms, asking me to forgive him. His face was hot and red; he looked so small and miserable, and so precious. I saw his love in his eyes; I felt his love in his body pressed against my own. And how my love went out to him! If I can have him back but five minutes, I want to take him back as that little penitent boy."

A man came to the church and asked to see the minister.

"Do you think God would be willing to have me in the church?" he said. "I've been an awful sinner." The look on his face showed he was deeply penitent.

"No," was the immediate answer. "I do not think so—I know so! 'If we confess our sins, he is faithful and just to forgive.'"

Infinite favor to the infinitely ill-deserving! Does that sound like good news to you?

III

But there is even more to the grace of God than that. It not only gives you a clean slate for all the wrong of the past. It gets busy on your behalf and works with you to build a new life out of the ruins of the old.

Joseph Fort Newton spent some of his time in the First World War with the soldiers in the armies in Europe. One day he spoke to a large number of them and afterward invited them to stay for a question-and-answer period. Someone asked the question, "What is the grace of God?" Before Newton could answer, a medical officer from New Zealand spoke up.

"The grace of God," he said, "is to the moral and spiritual world what the mysterious, ever-active power of recovery, of healing, of re-creation is in nature. When we are wounded, all the forces of healing in the body are rushed to the spot to repair the damage. A doctor only arrests infection till they

124

arrive. So, in the spiritual world a power of healing, of re-cuperation, of renewal, is always at work—if we yield to it and know how to work with it. That is the grace of God."

That puts the matter about as well as anything I know. Back about the year 164 there lived in Rome a famous phy-sician named Galen. Doctor Galen once said, concerning his work of healing, "I dressed his wound, but God healed him." As the New Zealander put it, what the force of healing in the physical world is, so is grace in the moral and spiritual. That suggests the very words which Peter uses in the text. "The God of all grace . . . shall himself perfect, establish, strengthen you."

A sign in a shop window read, "No piece of crockery broken beyond repair." There is a sign in the window of heaven in the form of a cross, and it reads, "No life broken beyond repair." The grace of God not only forgives sin, but rushes to the place of moral need with a secret, silent power to heal and repair and restore.

A letter came in the mail one morning months ago. It had no name signed to it, and so I feel at liberty to quote it in full. "My husband will be in your congregation on Sunday morning. Please place your hand on this letter and pray that God will put into your mouth words that will touch his heart. Pray that he will be given strength to overcome the influence of evil companions, that he will be delivered from the woman who is wrecking him, that he will be brought to the realization that no happiness but only shame and dishonor can come of this for all concerned. Pray that he will be the kind, fine, up-right man he once was, that I will be forgiven and strength-ened wherein I have failed, and that Christ and peace and love will yet reign within our poor broken lives and home before it is too late."

Of course you know I did as she requested. I prayed that God would forgive the old sins and repair the broken lives and restore that home to peace and happiness. And I prayed in the confidence that God could and would answer that prayer, when given the chance; for I knew that God is the God of all grace.

O that I could share with you something of the meaning of this word "grace"! It may be you are carrying a heavy load of guilt. It may be you have been held so long in the iron grip of some habit like drink or dishonesty or infidelity that you despair of ever being your old self again. Would that you might know that, as strongly as you disbelieve in yourself, there is a God who still believes in you! Would that you might know that there is a God who forgives freely, who not only forgives but will come to you, if you will let him, with a secret, silent power of healing—to lift you up out of your discouragement and stand you on your feet and set you walking once again in the paths of uprightness and honor! Would that you might pray the prayer,

> And oh for a man to arise in me,
> That the man I am may cease to be!

and then help God answer that prayer for you!

I bid you, open your eyes and behold the great grace of God. Not only behold, but reach out your hand and take hold. Know for yourself "the God of all grace," who will "perfect, establish, strengthen you"!